Growing into Peace

Growing into Peace

A Manual for Peace-Builders in the 1990s and Beyond

by

Mary Perkins

GEORGE RONALD
OXFORD

GEORGE RONALD, Publisher
46 High Street, Kidlington, Oxford OX5 2DN
© Mary Perkins 1991
All Rights Reserved

British Library Cataloguing in Publication Data
Perkins, Mary
  Growing into peace: a manual for peace-builders in the 1990s and
  beyond.
  1. Peace
  I. Title
  327.172

ISBN 0-85398-323-2

Contents

Yet so it shall be;
these fruitless strifes, these ruinous wars
shall pass away,
and the 'Most Great Peace' shall come . . .[1]

Bahá'u'lláh

The human race, as a distinct, organic unit, has passed through evolutionary stages analogous to the stages of infancy and childhood in the lives of its individual members, and is now in the culminating period of its turbulent adolescence approaching its long-awaited coming of age.[2]

The Universal House of Justice

Walking for peace in Madagascar

I
CLEARING THE GROUND

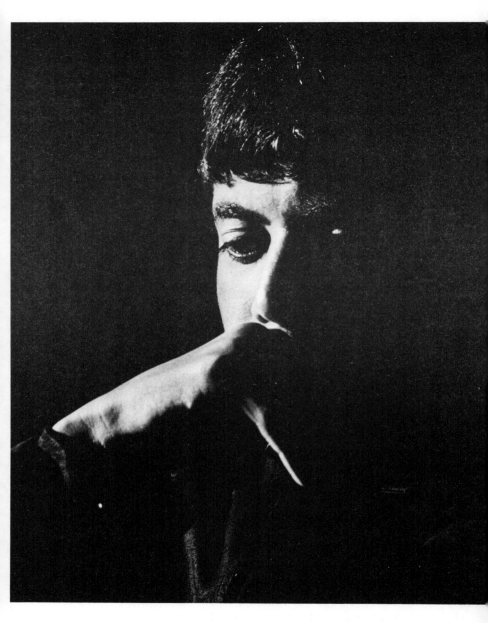

Will peace on earth ever be possible?

1

Introduction

WILL peace on earth ever be possible?

Can we begin to hope for a world without war, without a nuclear balance of terror and constant military preparedness?

As the old, rigid certainties of the Cold War era crumble, will new divisions and tensions inevitably arise? Will relations between nations always be based on rivalry and competition or can some new pattern of behaviour evolve?

Is there a chance that the nations of the world might cooperate to bring an end to famine, poverty and disease? Can they act together fast enough to prevent ecological catastrophe from engulfing us all? Will there be a future for our children and grandchildren?

Why are there still thousands of weapons of all kinds and millions of starving people?

How can one make any sense of it all and where will it all end?

Each person alive today at some point or other asks one or more of these questions. Sometimes the questions make us feel uncomfortable, unhappy or just downright scared. So we push them away to one side of our mind and go on with what seem to be more immediately urgent matters. But the questions don't go away and we need answers urgently.

Why are there so many problems – pollution, inflation, racism, poverty, violence, drugs – and why are we unable to solve them? Where should we start? And what can *one* person do? What kind of peace is possible in a world where half the people do not get enough to eat and where millions of lives are crippled by poverty? What is the use of thinking about world peace when our very future as a species is threatened by our own destruction of the environment? How can we hope for peace at the end of a century in which so many millions have died in wars? How can we even talk about peace in the world when there is so little peace in our hearts and homes, in our villages, towns and cities? Isn't it easier to conclude from the apparent evidence that human beings are incapable of learning any sense and that we are all doomed, sooner rather than later, to come to a nasty end?

The Bahá'í teachings give an emphatic and resounding 'no' to this counsel of despair. Over a century ago, while a prisoner and an exile, Bahá'u'lláh, the founder of the Bahá'í Faith, explained how peace would be established in the world. First, He said, would come a political armistice, an agreement by the nations of the world to abandon warfare as a means of settling their disputes. The armed and hostile nations of the world would be driven to this agreement, He explained, by economic pressures and the fear of mutual extinction. This political agreement He referred to as the Lesser Peace.

At the same time, Bahá'u'lláh explained, the roots of a deeper and more lasting peace would gradually be laid down. This peace, referred to by Bahá'u'lláh as the Most Great Peace, would be built from the ground up by ordinary men and women, youth and children. The roots of this peace, based on justice and trust, stretch far back into history, for it is no less than:

The Great Peace towards which people of good will throughout the centuries have inclined their hearts, of which seers and poets for countless generations have expressed their vision, and for which from age to age the sacred scriptures of mankind have constantly held the promise . . .[1]

World peace, Bahá'u'lláh explains, is not a utopian dream that will never be realized. It is a practical, attainable goal. It is within our reach, indeed, it is already being built, consciously or unconsciously, by millions of people all over the planet. Each one of us can help or hinder its realization.

Who was Bahá'u'lláh?

Bahá'u'lláh was the founder of the Bahá'í Faith. He was a Persian nobleman who lived in the last century. He claimed to be the bearer of a message from God which is for every individual on the planet. He spent the greater part of His life in exile and in prison because He brought a message of peace to a warring world. The Sháh of Persia and Sultán 'Abdu'l-'Azíz, the Ottoman Emperor, both of whom wielded absolute power in their respective realms, joined forces to suppress His teachings. They sentenced Him to isolated and perpetual imprisonment in a remote and terrible penal colony. They tortured and killed His followers and strove by every means in their power to eliminate the Bahá'í Faith from the face of the planet. They failed.

In the face of opposition and persecution Bahá'u'lláh continued to teach and to write. To the one Western scholar who took the trouble to visit Him in exile, He said:

. . . these fruitless strifes, these ruinous wars shall pass away, and the 'Most Great Peace' shall come. . . Do not you in Europe need this also? Is not this that which Christ foretold?[2]

There are now Bahá'ís, followers of Bahá'u'lláh, in almost

every corner of the globe. They find in the teachings of
Bahá'u'lláh hope and vision in a time of worldwide stress and
turmoil and a means of building peace in their hearts, their
homes and in the world, our common home.

In essence, the Bahá'í message is one of unity and the
removal of prejudice. 'The world', Bahá'u'lláh wrote, 'is but
one country, and mankind its citizens.'[3] The Bahá'í teachings
show how we can remove the root causes of war and violence
and build a just and lasting peace.

The peace of which Bahá'u'lláh writes is peace in both its
deepest and broadest senses: peace of mind and heart for
every individual and a condition of justice amongst the
nations and peoples of the world. The guidance that we now
need to achieve both internal and external peace is contained
in the Bahá'í teachings. These teachings will enable each one
of us to discover and use the peace-building capacities which
exist within us all.

2

A Special Time

A primary fact of the present world situation is that while the power to destroy the earth is concentrated in a few hands, the power to make and strengthen peace is widely dispersed.[1]

UN Secretary-General Perez de Cuellar, September 1988

WE are alive at a very special time in human history. Just as a twelve- or fourteen-year-old can accomplish tasks which are impossible for a five- or seven-year-old, so at this particular time in history humanity has developed the capacity to achieve many things which were utterly impossible in previous ages and centuries. The most significant but most often neglected of all these emerging capacities is our capacity for peace-building, the power and the tools that we now have to create a peaceful world. For the first time in all the centuries and millennia that human beings have existed, we have the capacity to create a peaceful, united world community of peoples and nations.

'Do not think the peace of the world an ideal impossible to attain!'[2] 'Abdu'l-Bahá writes. 'Warfare and strife will be uprooted, disagreement and dissension pass away and universal peace unite the nations and peoples of the world.'[3]

The first step to achieving anything involves coming to a

realization that what we would like to do is actually possible. How can we reach such a realization over the seemingly impossible task of achieving peace in the world? We can make a start by learning more about the process of peace-building and what we ourselves can contribute.

Peace-building is a process that involves each person alive today. Just as each human body is composed of a myriad individual cells, so too the body of the world of humanity is made up of more than five billion individual people. We now know that each of the myriad cells in the human body makes a unique and significant contribution to the total health or sickness of each human being. In the same way, each individual human being has a unique and vital contribution to make to the health and well-being of the whole body of humanity.

Discovering what peace-building is all about and finding out what we can do may be compared to a journey of exploration. In any interesting and worthwhile journey one does not instantly reach one's destination. In many areas of life today we have grown accustomed to expect 'instant' answers to our needs. We can press buttons and be supplied with an instant drink or a hot meal, an instant voice at the other end of a telephone, instant entertainment on a television or computer screen. Peace-building is the most urgent and important work to be done in the world today but it requires more effort, concentration and application than merely pushing buttons.

What we have to realize is that peace-building is a gradual and organic process. Peace will not be established overnight but we can definitely expect to see a speeding up of the peace-building process over the coming decade. Moreover, the sooner we understand what each one of us can do, the sooner will peace come. In addition, each journey of exploration and investigation is, in itself, part of the process of building a peaceful world. As we enlarge our understanding of what is involved in peace-building, as we discover the confidence and determination to act and find new 'tools' that we can use in our own lives, so each of us will be able to speed up the movement towards peace in the world.

What does peace mean to you now?

You can begin finding out what peace means to you by doing the following exercise. Take a blank sheet of paper, write peace in the centre and make a small circle around the word. Then draw lines out from the circle and write down in other circles at the end of the lines what peace means to you, in your home, at school or college, in your local community, in your country and in the world. Make connections between the circles where you can see that the issues are related to each other. Have fun – put down everything that you can think of.

When you can't think of anything more, go over the page again, underlining or putting stars by all the places where an increase in peacefulness depends on you doing something in a different way, or on you making an effort or taking an initiative.

In addition to understanding how you are involved in the process of peace-building, you may also realize from this exercise that peace-building is a complex process and must be perceived and understood from a variety of complementary angles. Writing a book about peace-building is rather like trying to fit a whole orange between the flat pages of a book. It would, in one sense, be easier if the whole book could be shaped like an orange with each chapter as a segment of the orange. But such a book would be both difficult to produce and to read and would take up a lot of space on a bookshelf. Also, when we take an orange to pieces, the separate parts of the fruit dry out, harden and shrivel up – unless of course we eat it quickly!

There is a wholeness, an interrelatedness to the complementary aspects of peace-building which is akin to the round, fragrant, smooth, sweet quality of a ripe but unpeeled orange. Because of the linear limitations of printed books, we shall consider, one by one, the complementary aspects of peace in separate chapters while continually being aware that it is easier to dissect an orange than it is to separate, one from another, the interrelated and closely interwoven aspects of the peace-building process.

3

Problem-Solving:
Three Essential Ingredients

THERE are three important steps to be taken in solving any problem. They apply in all situations whether the problem is large or small, whether it is a problem faced by all the world's peoples or by one single human being.

Knowledge

First of all, we have to *understand* exactly what is happening and why there is a problem. For instance, if your bicycle tyre goes flat while you are out cycling, you realize that air is leaking out. This is a sign or symptom that there is something wrong. You may be able to get home by stopping frequently and pumping more air into the tyre. But unless you take out the inner tube when you get home, find the hole and mend it, the problem will remain. If you try to ride the bike when the tyre is flat, you will ruin the tyre and maybe damage the wheel itself.

In the process of understanding, we have to distinguish between *symptoms* and *causes*. Doctors have to do this all the time. If they treat only the symptoms of a disease without finding out what is causing the illness, they may be able to relieve the patient's pain or discomfort for awhile. But unless they establish the cause or causes of the disease, they will not be able to begin to cure it. If they only treat symptoms without paying attention to the cause, the disease may break out at a later date even more fiercely than at first.

Often there is more than one cause of a problem. In considering the arms race, we can see that the enormous stockpiles of weapons, nuclear and conventional, are symptoms that something is wrong in the relations that presently exist among the nations of the world. While the reduction of armaments is a necessary part of reducing tension and the danger of nuclear war, these weapons are symptoms of deeper problems. We have to ask, what causes nations to think it necessary to have these weapons? Only by understanding the underlying causes shall we be able to take appropriate action.

Knowledge of what action would be appropriate to take is also essential. There must be a solution to hand and we must know what it is and how to apply it. We must also feel confident that the solution to the problem is possible. It is no use knowing that a particular medicine will make us well if the medicine is not available or we cannot afford it. That will not solve our problem. We need to know that there is a solution that is available to us, an action we *can* take.

The question as to where we can obtain reliable and accurate knowledge will be dealt with as we proceed. For the moment it is simply necessary to establish the principle that obtaining sound and reliable knowledge is the first and most vital step in problem-solving.

Will

This is the second step in solving a problem, which must

follow the acquisition of knowledge. Accurate knowledge of a problem and having a solution available will not be any use if the element of *will* or determination is lacking. For instance, if you know that your bike has a puncture and you have a bike repair kit in your pocket but can't be bothered to mend the puncture, you won't get very far next time you need your bike in a hurry. The element of will is also closely connected to your knowledge of the problem and your confidence in your understanding of it. Someone who is sick will not be willing to take medicine prescribed by a doctor in whom he or she has little confidence.

Action

This is the third step in solving a problem. Our *action* must be based on accurate knowledge of the nature and cause of the problem. Action to solve the problem must be connected to knowledge, it springs from it. If it does not spring from this knowledge, it may not only fail to solve the problem but may cause all kinds of further complications and trigger other problems while the original problem goes untreated and often gets worse.

Once we know what the problem is and we know how to solve it and we decide to do something, we must *act*.

Conclusion

These are the three steps we must take in problem-solving. If any one of the three steps is missing we will not succeed in solving a problem. If we don't understand the cause of the problem we won't know the action needed to solve it. If we are not willing to carry out the appropriate action, we won't solve the problem. If we do not act, the problem remains unsolved.

'Abdu'l-Bahá wrote:

> The attainment of any object is conditioned upon knowledge, volition and action. Unless these three conditions are forthcoming there is no execution or accomplishment.[1]

We must pay equal attention to all three elements of problem-solving. Although we start with knowledge, we must give just as much attention to will and action. If any one of the elements is weak, for instance, if we don't have a clear understanding of what is wrong, if we don't have enough determination to overcome obstacles which may arise, or if we only put into practice part of the solution, the problem will remain unsolved.

You can use this plan for problem-solving to examine problems you have encountered in the past in your own life or which you are encountering at present. Which of the three elements do you already have and which are you lacking? As you begin to do this you will realize that problem-solving is something that involves the whole of your being if you are to obtain knowledge, summon up will-power and determination and then carry out the necessary action.

4

The Human Problem

KNOWLEDGE, will and action must go together; they are three inseparable elements in problem-solving. The principle of wholeness which this fact demonstrates is equally important when we begin to consider the problems which the nations of the world face at the present time. It has become clear to those already involved in peace-building that the various perils that now threaten our future and the future of all life on earth are not separate issues but are related aspects of one central problem.

A reductionist method of analyzing problems – that is, a method whereby objects are dissected and split into parts so that each part may be observed and analyzed – was firmly established in Europe at the time of the scientific revolution and has been rigorously practised in western civilization since that time. It has been of enormous assistance in enabling us to increase our knowledge of the structure of the world and of all living organisms and is a necessary component of problem-solving. However, we have become so used to examining objects or issues one at a time, to reducing them to their smallest constituent parts and examining each part of these problems in microscopic detail that we have become unused to seeing them as 'wholes'.

We can see the reductionist tendency at work in the way we attempt to understand current world problems. We like to make lists, to categorize, to arrange in order of priority, to isolate and label processes, to pin each one down so that we can take it apart and find out what it consists of. Thus we have made headings in our minds – 'the arms race', 'hunger', 'the population explosion', 'developed countries' and 'developing countries', 'racism', 'pollution' and so on. We have groups of people who are working devotedly and often sacrificially on one or other of the problems listed for disarmament, human rights, ecology, civil rights, poverty action, status of women, the Third World and so on.

But a fragmented approach cannot, on its own, help us to understand the nature of the crisis that the world now faces and in our present extremity a new realization is dawning on us. In the scientific world the change in approach began to occur slowly in the first decades of this century as physicists began to explore the world of sub-atomic particles. As the physicist Fritjof Capra explains:

> The universe is no longer seen as a machine, made up of a multitude of objects, but has to be pictured as one indivisible dynamic whole whose parts are essentially interrelated and can be understood only as patterns of a cosmic process. . . sub-atomic particles have no meaning as isolated entities but can be understood only as interconnections or correlations between various processes of observation and measurement. . .
>
> This is how modern physics reveals the basic oneness of the universe. It shows that we cannot decompose the world into independently existing smallest units. As we penetrate into matter, nature does not show us any isolated basic building blocks but rather appears as a complicated web of relations between the various parts of a unified whole.[1]

Amongst people who are working for disarmament,

Poverty

Drought and famine

Violence in our cities

Natural disasters

Refugees

Environmental problems

The 'human problem' – a cluster of interconnected problems

Women grow 70% of the food in Africa

The education of women and girls is an essential element of development

development, women's rights, environmental issues, etc. a realization of the essential interconnectedness of the world's problems has now clearly emerged. When a very high proportion of the world's existing resources is devoted to military rivalry and preparedness, the problems of disarmament and development are inseparable. What you do with the resources of each country affects the ecology of that country and that of its neighbours. The nuclear threat, both from weapons and from power stations, is the most dangerous of the present ecological problems. The fact that women grow seventy per cent of the food in Africa means that the education, rights and status of women are essential elements of development. And so on.

In the early 1970s a group of the world's leading scientists, the Club of Rome, pooled their knowledge in a study of the present planetary problems. When they combined the insights gained from their separate disciplines they became aware that all the major world problems which we think of under separate headings are, in fact, so closely related as to be aspects of one problem. They called this cluster of worldwide interconnected problems 'the human problem' and concluded, after studying the problems from every angle, that:

Suddenly – virtually overnight when measured on a historical scale – mankind finds itself confronted by a multitude of unprecedented crises . . .
Real solutions are apparently interdependent, collectively the whole multitude of crises appears to constitute a single global crisis-syndrome of world development.[2]

The scientists drew attention to certain characteristics which all these interrelated problems share. Each problem affects everyone alive today in that each has a direct bearing on every aspect of all our lives. If considered separately, each one is a threat to human survival but not one of them can be solved in isolation from all the others. None of them are temporary crises and short-term temporary measures will not solve any of them but may only make matters worse. Furthermore, they cannot be solved by traditional, isolated and fragmentary actions. In other words, no country can solve any one of these problems in isolation either from other countries or in isolation from other aspects of the human problem. Finally, and most important, the scientists stated, these problems are not technological but ethical problems; in other words they have to do with values, what we think and believe about ourselves, about our relationship to other people on the planet and how we perceive the relationship of human beings to their natural environment.

One consequence of the firmly-established 'reductionist' scientific method and the incredible technological progress that it has triggered is that we are conditioned to search for technological answers to problems. Thus we look for technological solutions for our national fears and insecurities. We look to medical technology to solve problems of cholesterol-clogged arteries. We think that the first thing to be done to feed the world's hungry people is simply to produce more food.

But if we attempt this approach with problems that are in essence 'ethical problems', we cannot hope to succeed. The first essential, the scientists reported, is to see the problems in a global context and to develop a sense of world citizenship.

'This span of earth', Bahá'u'lláh wrote over a century ago, 'is but one homeland and one habitation.'[3]

5

Gaining a Perspective

How can we begin to make any sense of the extraordinary world we live in? No previous generation of earth-dwellers has lived at a time of such extreme and spectacular contradictions. In no previous era have people all over the planet longed so desperately for peace and security but at no other time have people been so busy preparing to ensure their mutual destruction. At no other time have people in one part of the world cared so much and worked so hard to help others less fortunate than themselves but in no other century have there been so many people dying of entirely avoidable diseases caused by poverty and want.

No previous inhabitants of spaceship earth have ever had the chance to see the earth as we have seen it on our television screens – a breathtakingly lovely sphere swathed in wreaths of cloud. No other people have ever acquired the knowledge that we now have about our planet, its upper atmospheres and ozone layers, its fiery heart and its ocean depths, its fragile and intricate ecosystem. Yet no other people have ever engaged in such massive destruction of forest and farmland, such spoliation of lakes, rivers and seas, such fouling of the air we all must breathe, such rapid annihilation of so many species of plants and animals.

Bewildered and confused by these contradictions, we need a place from which we can try to get a view of all that is happening so that we can begin to understand it. We need to find a vantage point from which we can gain some perspective, just as a traveller lost in a forest needs a hill onto which he can climb so that he can survey his surroundings and find out where he is.

The most important clue to understanding our present dilemma can be found in a sentence written by Shoghi Effendi, the Guardian of the Bahá'í Faith. He wrote in 1941, while the Second World War was raging:

> What we witness at the present time . . . is the adolescent stage in the slow and painful evolution of humanity, preparatory to the attainment of . . . the stage of maturity . . . The ages of its infancy and childhood are past, never again to return.[1]

All analogies are limited simply because the two things which are being compared are not identical. Obviously the collective history of the human race is not the same thing as an individual human life, but a comparison of the two processes will lead us to a deeper understanding of the present situation in the world.

Adolescence

Adolescence is the period of life between childhood and maturity, a time of rapid physical growth and development. Our bodies have to prepare for the responsibilities of adulthood, for the capacity to have children and the ability to support ourselves and others by earning our own livelihood. Emotionally it is also a time of rapid development but during this overall growth we can experience violent swings of emotion, feelings of joy and exhilaration which alternate with

Adolescence is a time of rapid physical growth and development

We need to find out what our purpose is in life

moods of despair and misery. Intellectually we begin to ask deeper questions about ourselves and the world around us, for we need a wider frame of reference than the one we accepted in childhood. We need to find out what our purpose is in life and discover how to use our new energy and strength in a way that will be satisfying and meaningful. We strive to be independent of our parents and to establish a relationship with them in which there is more awareness of our increasing maturity, but at times we simply revert to a childish pattern of behaviour. Because we have not yet reached maturity we feel insecure, and to compensate for this insecurity we compete with others in order to gain their respect and assert our own identity.

Inevitably, this time of rapid growth is a time of stress. It can be a bewildering time, our fast-growing bodies, our strong and swiftly-changing emotions and the new questions raised in our minds all make new and challenging demands. One thing is very clear though: even if we occasionally revert to childish habits, the books, the activities and the clothes of childhood no longer meet our needs. We are in the process of leaving childhood behind and of growing towards a new state of being.

The adolescence of humanity

If we start to think about the signs and symptoms evident in the life of the world, we can observe that over the last couple of centuries –

– we have increased our knowledge of the workings of our own bodies and of the physical structure of our planet and of the universe to a level previously unknown in human history;

– this increase in knowledge has led to an astonishing growth in human technological capacity. We have enormously increased our capacity to alter our own environment and we have more than sufficient strength to destroy it completely in a very short time;

— we have increased our capacity to feel for the sufferings of others both in our own societies and in distant countries but during the same period we have inflicted pain and suffering on millions of our fellow human beings on a scale unknown in previous centuries;

— the pace at which new discoveries are made and technologies developed is itself quickening ever more rapidly so that there are now more changes in the lifetime of a single person than in the span of several earlier centuries. If you know the year or the decade in which your grandparents were born, you can discover how very different the world was in their youth from the world in which you are growing up.

These signs and symptoms show us that there is a process of change going on. When we can see that everything around us in nature is in perpetual motion and change, it would be rather strange to find that the development of human society was exempt from this process. The Universal House of Justice, the supreme governing body of the Bahá'í Faith, has described the process of change and development of human society in this way:

> The human race, as a distinct, organic unit, has passed through evolutionary stages analogous to the stages of infancy and childhood in the lives of its individual members, and is now in the culminating period of its turbulent adolescence approaching its long-awaited coming of age.[2]

6

A Dilemma and a Challenge

WHILE individuals have passed from childhood to maturity since the beginning of human history, no previous generations have had to live through such a turbulent and critical phase in humanity's collective adolescence. All young people today face a unique dilemma and challenge, for never before in human history have there been so many varied dangers threatening the lives of individuals and societies.

From every direction we hear news bulletins or read headlines which remind us of the peril of our planet. Even the use of a tiny percentage of the nuclear weapons that are now stockpiled would devastate the earth. There is the alarming danger of nuclear proliferation, as more and more nations acquire the technical capacity to produce nuclear weapons. There is a constant risk of large-scale, deadly accidents occurring at nuclear power stations sited in different parts of the world. Then there are chemical, biological and laser weapons. There are the ever-increasing threats of chemical pollution and environmental destruction, ozone depletion, sewage-choked seas, acid lakes and dying forests. We are at a place where humanity has never been before, the dangers are increasing and there appears to be no way out. From early childhood we carry on our shoulders the weight of the planet's peril and wake every morning to a fresh bombardment of bad news from all over the world.

Sometimes the pain and distress we experience is so agonizing that we try to block it out completely, to pull down a shutter in our minds, to deny that it even exists, for it is all more, it seems, than we can possibly be expected to cope with. But such denial carries great costs, both emotional and intellectual. The pain we feel for our planet is a measure of our caring. When we block it out, we also block our own capacity for creative thought.

This pain, this planetary anguish we all feel, whether consciously or unconsciously, is itself a sign of growth and of hope. It is an inescapable rite of passage, part of our initiation into our collective adulthood. For us, for the first time in human history, there is no assurance of continuity. We know that we can extinguish life on our planetary home through fear, stupidity, greed or simple thoughtlessness.

In her book entitled *Despair and Personal Power in the Nuclear Age* Joanna Macy explains that our willingness to acknowledge our pain for the world is an essential first step in acquiring the power we need to heal its ills. She refers to a French editor, Gerard Blanc, who:

> points out that in adolescence we internalize the reality of personal death, and so-called primitive societies formalize this stage through rituals offering access to the rights and responsibilities of adulthood. Blanc wonders if humanity, in our planetary journey, has not reached a comparable stage, since we perceive, for the first time in our history, the possibility of our death as a species. Facing our despair and anguish for our world is, in effect, a kind of initiatory rite, necessary to our growing up – to the fulfilment of the promise within us.[1]

It is essential to acknowledge our feelings for the state of the planet, to share them with others and allow them to help us grow to a new sense of power, both individually and as a world community. This new, and often terrifying, awareness we have of what human beings can do and are doing to the planet and to all other living things has a purpose. It can evoke in us the capacity for parenthood. Whether or not we raise individual children of our own is here irrelevant. By our present actions or inactions we are, each one of us, shaping the world of the next century. The reality and the challenge of our time is that together we are moving towards maturity. The process of growth and transformation is never pain-free. The journey on which we are all embarked of traversing adolescence requires that we let go of outmoded ways of thinking and acting and actively strive to find new ways of living in peace with each other and in harmony with our environment.

Adolescence is a time of stress but it is also, and most important, a time of rapidly increasing capacity and strength. It is a time when we have to take on more responsibility for our own thoughts and actions. If we suddenly discover that a source of guidance exists either that we have never heard of or that most people have not considered seriously, then it is necessary to make a thorough investigation. Such a thing is too important and urgent to be ignored and we should not rely or depend on the opinions and answers of others.

It is a considerable relief to know that there is a road map with clear signposts which we can follow. It has existed for over a hundred years. It is contained in the Bahá'í writings. In the 1860s, while in exile Bahá'u'lláh wrote a series of letters to all the kings and rulers of the world, both secular and religious, outlining the steps necessary for establishing peace. His letters were ignored. The only slightly positive comment was made by Queen Victoria who is reported to have said on receiving her letter, 'If this is of God, it will endure, if not, it is of no matter.'

The Bahá'í Faith has done a lot more than endure in the century and a half since it began. It is now established in over one hundred and sixty countries. It is a worldwide community of individuals representative of most of the planet's diverse peoples. Its literature has been translated into almost 800 different languages. Yet its teachings are relatively little-known to most people and the extraordinary relevance of these teachings to the problems of our times has been largely overlooked.

One of the claims made in these writings is that war, violence and exploitation are not permanent and enduring characteristics of human society. They are adolescent traits, expressions of our collective immaturity. We shall leave them behind as we move from adolescence to maturity.

7

The Need to Know

'PEACE, we need peace, let it begin with me!' is the opening line of a popular song and, indeed, the process must begin with each one of us.

'Peace', 'Abdu'l-Bahá explains, 'must first be established among individuals, until it leadeth in the end to peace among nations.'[1]

To find out how peace may be established between individuals we must take a further step and discover how it may be established within an individual. We must discover how we may achieve peace and harmony within ourselves.

Every young person needs to discover who or what he or she really is and why he or she exists. This exploration is an essential part of growing to maturity. If the quest is not undertaken an individual may live through years or decades of discontent and dissatisfaction. The need for self-knowledge and the establishment of an identity is today paralleled by an urgent need to establish the causes of violence and war. The need for this knowledge is more urgent than it has ever been before as the future of all life on the planet is now in question.

There have been so many wars for so long, and the level of violence has increased to such a height in recent decades, that many people have sadly and reluctantly come to the conclusion that human beings are innately aggressive creatures. Many people are now certain that an 'aggressive instinct' is somehow programmed into human genes and that this innate aggressiveness is the essential driving force which determines the lives of individuals and nations.

How often have you heard someone say: 'There have always been wars and there always will be. Look at how many are going on right now! That's the way people are made, that's human nature, you can't change that!' This is a very widespread and firmly-held view. But is it really true?

We need an answer urgently for a number of reasons. In the first place, there could be no more certain way of continuing wars than a belief that they are inevitable. Secondly, if this belief in our 'innate aggressiveness' is not sound, it is hindering us from examining the real causes of war and violence. On the other hand, if there is an aggressive element in our nature which cannot be removed, we must always, both in our own home communities and in our relationships with other countries, provide the means by which it may be sublimated, released or safely expressed. If this is the case, must we accept that this will always be necessary, that we must just make the best of a bad deal, or can we be more hopeful and constructive?

The contradictions that we seem to carry within ourselves have exercised the minds of philosophers and artists for centuries. Shakespeare makes Hamlet ponder on the nobility and dignity of humanity: 'What a piece of work is a man! How noble in reason! how infinite in faculties, in form and moving how express and admirable! In action, how like an angel! In apprehension how like a god'[2]; while King Lear, on meeting with the raggedly-dressed Edgar, considers humanity from the opposite viewpoint: 'Is man no more than this? Consider him well . . . Thou art the thing itself, unaccommodated man is no more but such a poor, bare, forked animal as thou art.'[3]

We now know a great deal more about the workings of the

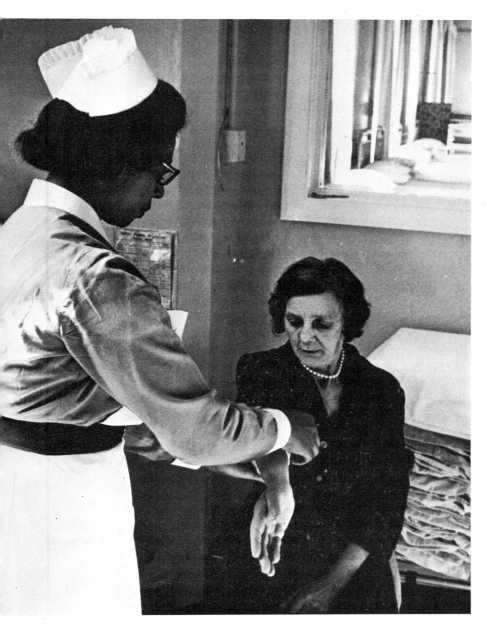

Which is the more basic and powerful — the tendency to act aggressively or to cooperate and nurture?

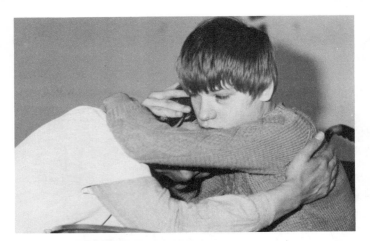

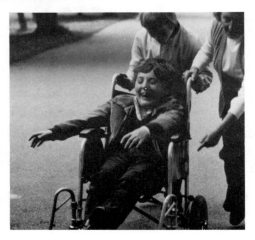

human body and brain than was known in Shakespeare's time
but we have such an abundance of information that it is very
difficult to pick our way through it. The evidence we can
gather from what is happening around us is confusing.
Bookstores and libraries are well stocked with popular
volumes presenting human beings as fundamentally selfish
and aggressive creatures whose lives are determined by strong
territorial instincts. At the same time, we all know of
individuals who have cared throughout their lives selflessly for
others, for the sick, the handicapped and the deprived,
sometimes in their own home areas but often half a world
away, amongst people of a different skin colour and nationality.

Which, we must enquire, is the more basic and most
powerful of these two opposing tendencies, the tendency to act
aggressively or to cooperate and nurture? Are we trapped in a
perpetual, terrifying seesaw between them? Or are we, as the
evidence of our eyes and ears might lead us to conclude,
simply schizophrenic?

When we start to think about world peace, we find this
same mixture of confusion and contradiction within our own
hearts and minds. We long for peace and security but in our
innermost thoughts and feelings we doubt it is possible. This
inner condition is reflected in the outer world where hostile
nations, supplied with enough weapons for a massive overkill
of all the world's peoples, constantly proclaim themselves to
be peace-loving nations.

'The world is in great turmoil,' Bahá'u'lláh wrote'and the
minds of its people are in a state of utter confusion.'[4]

Dr Richard Leakey, an anthropologist working in East
Africa, is one of a number of scientists who have queried the
pessimistic view of human nature. He writes:

> Homo sapiens, the argument runs, is innately aggressive, a
> 'killer-ape', and as technology becomes ever more refined,
> the military machine will grow in sophistication and

destructive power, and it will *be* used. If this argument is correct, then there appears to be very little one can do about it, for the holocaust will come sooner or later. But I am convinced that it is not correct, and that this popular notion of the 'killer-ape' is one of the most dangerous and destructive ideas mankind has ever had.[5]

How is it that this notion of 'innate aggressiveness' has taken such a hold on our minds? What can we do to establish its truth or falsity?

We must begin by asking several basic questions. What do we really know of ourselves? What do we mean when we use the phrase 'human nature'? Where do we get our ideas from and are they sound? What exactly is a human being? Are we just bundles of unconscious urges and reflexes neatly enclosed in separate skins? Are we merely biochemical processes? Are we fallen angels or are we particularly intelligent and destructive animals? What is the relationship between humanity and the rest of the material creation?

8

The Reality of Man

IN the Bahá'í writings we can find a more specific and detailed account of what a human being is and a more detailed explanation of our relationship to the rest of creation – both the visible material world and the invisible world of spirit – than is available elsewhere. This will be our starting point in the search for a deeper knowledge of ourselves.

The Bahá'í perspective

We can only begin to understand the reality of man and the phenomenon of human nature when we consider human beings in their total environment, that is, in relationship both to the invisible world of the spirit and to the world of physical creation.

Bahá'ís believe that the universe has 'a Creator, a Vivifier, a Provider, an Architect'[1] whom we call God, but that all that we attempt to say, write and think of God cannot describe Him. 'He is, and hath ever been, immensely exalted beyond all that can either be recounted or perceived.'[2]

Although the reality of God is beyond the grasp of the human mind, all that He has created reveals to us His signs or attributes. Thus, His Godhood reveals to us not only the perfection of fatherhood but the perfection of motherhood also: creating, providing for, nurturing, loving and guiding the whole creation. The universe, in all its vastness and intricacy, reveals this love, for it came into being because of the love of God. 'The cause of the creation of the phenomenal world is love.'[3] 'Love is the most great law that ruleth this mighty and heavenly cycle, the unique power that bindeth together the divers elements of this material world . . .'[4]

The material creation

All created things are linked to one another, 'Abdu'l-Bahá explains, 'by a linkage complete and perfect, even, for example, as are the members of the human body',[5] and 'every part of the universe is connected with every other part by ties that are very powerful and admit of no imbalance, nor any slackening whatever.'[6]

In the physical world we can identify with our physical senses several layers of creation, or planes of existence, which are often summarized as the mineral, vegetable and animal kingdoms. We can see in these three tiers a rising level of complexity. The mineral kingdom demonstrates the quality of cohesion, the vegetable kingdom possesses this quality but is also able to reproduce itself, while the animal kingdom possesses the qualities of both lower kingdoms and has in addition a nervous system which makes possible the power of movement and the development of intelligence.

The human spirit

The level immediately above the animal kingdom is that of the human kingdom. Human beings possess in themselves all the qualities of the lower kingdoms but partake of a spiritual reality which does not exist in the three lower levels. This human spirit or soul, as it is often called, is the very essence of our humanity.

Our physical body, which is the manifestation of our material or animal nature, we inherit from our parents' bodies and from the genes that their bodies carry. It is these genes which will determine our physical characteristics, whether we are tall or short, have blue eyes or brown, and so on. However, we are, each one of us, a unique physical creation unlike any other human being which has existed in the past or which will exist in the future, as our individual fingerprints attest.

Our spiritual being, which we call our soul or spirit, is also a unique creation, unlike any other soul that has ever existed or will ever exist.

'The soul is', Bahá'u'lláh writes, 'a sign of God, a heavenly gem whose reality the most learned of men hath failed to grasp, and whose mystery no mind, however acute, can ever hope to unravel.'[7]

While we are not able to unravel the mystery of the soul, certain aspects of its reality are described in the Bahá'í writings. The soul comes into existence at the time of physical conception, but does not 'inherit' characteristics in the way that our physical body does. Although the way that our parents raise us will affect the way our character or personality develops, the soul itself does not carry inherited traits nor will it decay or disintegrate as the body is bound, eventually, to do. The body, being composed of temporal, perishable, material elements, is subject to the same laws of growth and decay as the rest of the physical creation – in fact, the physical body reaches a growth peak when a person is in his late twenties or early thirties. Sometime after this, as a natural part of aging, calcium begins to be lost from bones and the physical body begins, very gradually, to deteriorate.

The soul, however, is something entirely different. It cannot be seen or perceived with any of our physical senses and no surgeon will ever find a soul within a human body:

> The soul is not a combination of elements, it is not composed of many atoms . . . It is entirely out of the order of the physical creation; it is immortal![8]

The mystery of how the human spirit is connected to the soul is, as yet, beyond our grasp: we can only make a comparison which may increase our understanding. The body is like a mirror which reflects the light of the soul. The light is not contained within the actual mirror and should the mirror be cracked or broken, the light itself will continue to shine.

Although the soul cannot be seen or perceived by any of our physical senses and is therefore impossible to describe in material terms, it nevertheless exists and possesses its own faculties. These are not physical faculties such as are provided by our eyes and ears but are spiritual capacities possessed by every single human being, including the capacity to be in touch with a level of reality above that of the physical world. 'Nature is not in touch with the realm of God,' 'Abdu'l-Bahá tells us, but through the faculties of his soul, 'man is attuned to its evidences'.[9]

This spiritual capacity was potential in humanity from the earliest times, just as the potential and capacity of a mature adult is present in the microscopic cluster of cells in which a new life begins to grow in a human womb. As the human embryo slowly develops through various shapes and forms while in the womb, so too the body of man passed through a series of evolutionary stages until it was possible for its latent spiritual capacity to manifest itself clearly. We shall, in a later chapter, explore the means by which this latent spiritual potential existing in every human being has been and continues to be developed, but for now we will continue with a brief overview of our biological inheritance.

Our biological inheritance

Our bodies have been subjected to the same evolutionary processes that all other forms of animal life have experienced, and through a complex process of mutation and selection they have evolved from simpler to more complex organisms over a period of billions of years. The biologists who discovered the DNA and RNA molecules in the 1950s revealed to us our close relationship with the rest of the material creation. Our bodies are made of the same basic components as are the rest of the creatures of the planet. There is a universal genetic code which runs, like a common thread, through all living creatures, and each species represents a slight variation of this theme. It might be possible therefore, in theory at least, to draw an imaginary unbroken line of descent from the first bacterium or single-celled organism in which animate life first appeared, to any individual human being or animal alive today. This relatedness provides strong evidence that all living creatures have evolved from a common ancestral form of life. The underlying unity and interconnectedness of all creatures might be thought of as 'the primal oneness deposited at the heart of all created things'.[10]

We possess similar powers of movement and the same senses of sight, hearing, smell and touch as can be found in other animals but in creatures other than man these powers and senses are often more powerful and more highly developed. We share with all other forms of animal life certain basic physical needs for food, warmth, shelter and security.

Our closest biological relatives

The DNA of chimpanzees differs by only 1.2% from the DNA of human beings. The difference in DNA between chimpanzees and orangutans is 2.2%. We are, therefore, in this respect, more closely related to chimpanzees than chimpanzees themselves are related to their primate cousins, the orangutans.

Recent studies of chimpanzees in the wild have revealed that chimpanzee and human societies share certain social features which are related to physical survival. The emotional bonds which begin to form at birth between chimpanzee infants and their mothers are strong and enduring. Chimpanzees also enjoy a long period of juvenile dependence and adults take it upon themselves to guard the young from danger, thus allowing them time to play and learn, through exploration of their environment and imitation of adults, the skills they will need in adult life. It has also been observed that fear and anxiety inhibit both the emotional and mental development of young chimpanzees. There are uncanny similarities in the way postures and gestures are used by both species for non-verbal communication and in the way that both humans and chimpanzees express certain basic emotions.

Laboratory research into the ingelligence of chimpanzees has shown that chimps are, if they know that they will be rewarded with food or a grooming session:

> . . . capable of considerable mental prowess: task learning based on insight, on the principles of arithmetic and on discrimination, symbolic communication, the efficient planning of a food-gathering itinerary and the ability to communicate the location of hidden foods to other chimpanzees.[11]

Moreover, certain individual chimpanzees held in captivity have sometimes repeated over and over again tasks they have been taught, apparently just for the satisfaction they derive from performing these tasks. They have been observed to work for several minutes on end with intense concentration for no material reward. Chimpanzees have remarkable memories not only for people and places but for symbols they have been

Chimpanzee and human societies share certain social features

The differences which separate us from the great apes must be identified at the spiritual level

taught to use in sign language. They can recognize themselves in mirrors and have a highly developed ability to interpret photographs.

Our close physical relationship to chimpanzees, the striking similarities in the social behaviour of the two species and the remarkable powers of intelligence possessed by chimpanzees and the other great apes have led many people to conclude that the differences which separate us from our primate cousins are of degree only and not of kind. Bahá'ís, however, consider that the differences which separate us from the great apes and the rest of the animal kingdom must be identified at the spiritual level. Clearly, our bodies are part of the material creation but the spiritual gifts with which we are endowed enable us to rise above the limitations of an animal existence. Similarly, the misuse or neglect of these spiritual gifts can lead us to behave more ferociously, cruelly and destructively than any animal.

We cannot place our souls under microscopes nor examine any aspect of our spiritual reality as we can our bodies, but an examination of the conclusions reached by an eminent scientist, Dr Jane Goodall, who has studied chimpanzees in the wild for over twenty-five years, provides significant clues to the nature of our unique human reality.

How we differ from chimpanzees

In the conclusion to her detailed and enthralling study of the chimpanzees of Gombe in Tanzania, Dr Goodall expresses the view that 'even if we do differ from the apes not in kind, but only in degree, that degree is still overwhelmingly large. . .'[12] She explains that '. . . knowledge of the ways in which our behaviour is *similar* to that of the chimpanzee, combined with knowledge of how it is *different*, helps us, I believe, to pinpoint what it is that makes man unique.'[13]

Dr Goodall draws attention to three significant differences in human and chimpanzee behaviour. The first is the human development of a rich spoken language, a topic we shall explore in more detail in a later chapter. Secondly, she calls attention to our capacity to overcome, by conscious choice, the selfish impulses of our biological inheritance. Thirdly, she stresses our superior capacity to understand the suffering that our actions can cause to other living creatures.

Conclusion

Whether one approaches this topic with the view that the differences separating us from the apes are of degree only, albeit an overwhelmingly large degree, or with the view that there is a difference in kind, the conclusion reached is strikingly similar. Human beings have choices of action which are not open to animals and are possessed of a capacity unequalled in the animal creation to appreciate the pain and suffering that we are capable of inflicting on each other and all creatures.

'Abdu'l-Bahá writes of the nature of man in these words:

> In man there are two natures; his spiritual or higher nature and his material or lower nature. In one he approaches God, in the other he lives for the world alone. . .[14]

> Man is in the highest degree of materiality and at the beginning of spirituality – that is to say, he is the end of imperfection and the beginning of perfection. He is at the last degree of darkness, and at the beginning of light . . . Not in any other of the species in the world of existence is there such a difference, contrast, contradiction and opposition as in the species of man.[15]

9

A Unique Predicament

IN this chapter we shall explore in more detail the contrasts and contradictions that characterize the human condition and see how these relate to our unique spiritual endowment. For a start, we can remind ourselves of the major ways in which we can easily be distinguished from our nearest biological relatives, the higher primates, and from all other animals.

We are the only primates who have developed the capacity to walk habitually on two legs instead of four.

Our brains are larger in relation to our bodies than those of all but one other mammal: 'Man's brain size now deviates from the mammalian norm to an extent which is shared only by the bottle-nosed dolphin.'[1]

Human beings are, at birth, the most helpless of all living creatures. Most week-old animals can not only walk but run as well. Human babies learn to walk when they are about a year old and need the support and care of parents or other adults longer than any other species.

Although a few animals use natural objects as tools to help them obtain food, no animal makes such far-reaching changes to natural objects as do humans. As Richard Leakey explains, 'When a human being turns a natural object into a tool . . . the finished product often looks nothing like the raw material.

No animal makes tools in the imaginative way that humans do.'[2]

We communicate with each other by means of a rich and complex spoken language. While the higher primates communicate through gestures, movements, signs and a variety of sounds, this communication comes nowhere near the richness and complexity of human speech. Exciting new efforts to communicate with chimpanzees and gorillas have resulted in humans and apes communicating through sign language. But this involves the concentrated use of both eyes and hands simultaneously. The advantage of human speech is that it involves only our mouths and ears, leaving our eyes and hands free for other activities.

The development of a spoken language has meant that we are able to pass on not only practical skills but acquired knowledge and traditions of thought from one generation to another. Animals can pass on knowledge and skills acquired in dealing with their environment but nothing more. The capacity first to create culture and then to hand it on to future generations arose in large part through the uniqueness of human speech.

In a biological sense, the world is for human beings 'one homeland and one habitation'[3] for we have taken one giant evolutionary step further than any other animal. Instead of simply adapting our bodies and our ways of living to suit our environment, we have developed an ability to alter our environment to suit ourselves. But, at the end of the twentieth century, we have reached a point where this adaptation of the environment for our own short-term convenience presents a threat to all life on the planet, our own included. Although we have devised ways and means of living anywhere on the planet, we too are a part of nature and we are just as dependent on a healthy environment as are all other living creatures. Yet today we are the greatest threat to all species and to the planet itself, for we are the one species that can

Our brains are larger in relation to our bodies than those of all but one other mammal — the bottle-nosed dolphin

'No animal makes tools in the imaginative way that humans do'

bring to sudden extinction the myriad life forms that have evolved on our planetary home.

No other living species is as intelligent as we are, yet no other species has indulged for so long in such unrestrained and widespread aggression, violence and destruction. In the animal kingdom there is, of necessity, a struggle for survival. Animals hunt and kill animals of other species in order to eat and thus live. But while in nature all things are eaters and eaten, we alone have harnessed the earth's vast resources for the express purpose of slaughtering one another. Our knowledge and skills have brought us to the very brink of a terrifying abyss of total destruction. Even as we teeter precariously on the edge of this abyss, our everyday, 'civilized' way of life degrades, abuses, pollutes and destroys the natural environment on which we depend. Human beings are now destroying other species at a rapidly increasing rate.

Can we step back from the abyss? Can we stop the wholesale destruction and discover ways of living in harmony with each other and with other creatures?

Yes, we can, for we are not simply highly intelligent and particularly destructive animals. We are endowed with unique and extraordinary capacities for understanding the processes of the natural world and we have the power to nurture, protect and enhance the diversity of life on earth.

'The Almighty', 'Abdu'l-Bahá has written,

> hath not created in man the claws and teeth of ferocious animals, nay rather hath the human form been fashioned and set with the most comely attributes and adorned with the most perfect virtues. The honour of this creation and the worthiness of this garment therefore require man to have love and affinity for his own kind, nay rather to act towards all living creatures with justice and equity.[4]

We need to learn more about these capacities. We need to understand who and what we are before we can begin to act effectively. Our long absorption in what we can do and make has caused us to neglect our inner, spiritual selves but as 'Abdu'l-Bahá warns:

> No matter how far the material world advances, it cannot establish the happiness of mankind. Only when material and spiritual civilization are linked and coordinated will happiness be assured.[5]

The terrifying predicament in which we now find ourselves can only be understood, and therefore can only be solved, when we have obtained a deeper understanding of our unique spiritual endowment.

A spiritual endowment

'God has', 'Abdu'l-Bahá explains 'created all earthly things under a law of progression in material degrees, but He has created man and endowed him with powers of advancement toward spiritual and transcendental kingdoms.'[6]

The clue to understanding our nature is to be found in these 'powers of advancement' which the human soul possesses.

'From among all created things', Bahá'u'lláh wrote, 'He [God] hath singled out for His special favour the pure, the gem-like reality of man, and invested it with a unique capacity of knowing Him and of reflecting the greatness of His glory.'[7]

The capacity to know and to love are not so much two separate capacities as two inseparable aspects of our spiritual being. As we are unable to unravel the mystery of the soul, so even our language and concepts are inadequate to describe its essence and nature. Even thinking of knowing and loving as separate capacities creates an artificial barrier in our minds for we immediately make a division between 'head' and 'heart', between 'intellect' and 'intuition' which diminishes our wholeness.

Because we have often misunderstood their interdependence and because we are so used to taking things apart and putting labels on them, we think and speak about our heads and hearts pulling in opposite directions. However, a moment's reflection will cause us to realize that both these functions are carried out by the human mind. When attempting to describe our capacity to acquire knowledge we make a further subdivision between 'intellect' and 'intuition' but both are aspects of the gift of understanding which, Bahá'u'lláh explained, '. . . giveth man the power to discern the truth in all things, leadeth him to that which is right, and helpeth him to discover the secrets of creation.'[8]

The essential interdependence of loving and knowing is also illustrated by 'Abdu'l-Bahá: 'All things are beneficial if joined with the love of God; and without His love all things are harmful.'[9]

If one aspect of our spiritual capacity is neglected while the other is developed, an unevenness in life arises which manifests itself as a lack of balance and harmony within both individuals and societies. Bearing in mind this essential interdependence of loving and knowing, we shall now consider each aspect in more detail.

The capacity to know

'Abdu'l-Bahá gives a useful definition of a human being. Man is, He states:

> the highest specialized organism of visible creation, embodying the qualities of the mineral, vegetable and animal plus an ideal endowment absolutely minus and absent in the lower kingdoms – the power of intellectual investigation into the mysteries of outer phenomena.[10]

It is this power of discovery which distinguishes human beings from all other species and places us in a unique relationship with our environment, enabling us either to enhance it or destroy it completely. No other species has such power. While animals explore their environment with the aid of their senses, are endowed with feelings and do learn new ways of behaving which will help them to live more comfortably and success- fully, they do not possess man's 'conscious power of penetrating abstract realities'.[11] 'Abdu'l-Bahá explains that 'the exalta- tion of the animal world is to possess perfect members, organs and powers, and to have all its needs supplied'[12] but man is endowed 'with a mighty power which is capable of discovering the mysteries of phenomena'.[13] By first making observations with the aid of the physical senses and then bringing into play the powers of the intellect, man is able to bring to light previously unknown facts.

This capacity for intellectual investigation may be thought of as a glass through which the light of a higher realm lights the material world. 'It is', 'Abdu'l-Bahá writes, 'the discoverer of the hidden and mysterious secrets of the material universe and is peculiar to man alone.'[14]

'Abdu'l-Bahá also states that while the intelligence of the animal remains at the same level, the human power of abstract thought increases century by century. It is this human endowment that has made our unique evolutionary development and the rise of civilizations possible and which enables us to discover our own history: This gift of God

> unites present and past, reveals the history of bygone nations and events, and confers upon man today the essence of all human knowledge and attainment throughout the ages.[15]

The capacity to love

Just as the human intellectual capacity transcends the limited learning capacity of animals, so too the human capacity to love is greater than that which exists in the animal kingdom. In both aspects the difference is not simply of degree but of kind. In *The Hidden Words*, Bahá'u'lláh, speaking as the Creator, says: 'O Son of the Wondrous Vision! I have breathed within thee a breath of My own Spirit, that thou mayest be My lover.'[16]

The human capacity to love includes the attachment, emotional bonding and group loyalties that exist in the higher primates but also has an extra and higher dimension specialized to humans alone: the capacity to care for all other human beings and living creatures. It is this transcendent quality, this capacity to live beyond the constraints of animal existence that has enabled people throughout history to risk their own lives in the service of others. It is this capacity which explains the paradox at the heart of human existence, that in reaching out towards our Creator and towards others we discover the core of our own being.

'Man is', 'Abdu'l-Bahá states, 'he who forgets his own interests for the sake of others.'[17]

This reaching out is a gradual process which takes place in each individual life and also in the evolution of human society. The gradual progress towards justice in human affairs represents the working out at a national and international level of this original creative principle of love.

Jane Goodall, in an interview with a British journalist, spoke of a significant difference between human and animal societies: 'The more I find close similarities with us, the more I realize too how great the gulf is between us. They have no moral sense: in chimp society only might is right.'[18]

Only when we live in harmony with the original and creative principles of love and knowledge will we be able to build lives that have an enduring meaning, that are concerned with more than mere physical satisfaction or even the handing on of our own particular genes. There is a basic human need to discover the spiritual purpose of one's life and to build a life around this purpose. As the Universal House of Justice has written, 'we need to know who we are and for what purpose we exist.'

Viktor Frankl, a leading psychologist who spent a number of years as a prisoner of war in Auschwitz, spent all the years after his release helping people to recognize their individual need to discover meaning and purpose. His thesis is that when this need is ignored or suppressed a state of disease is created in individuals which manifests itself in depression, addiction and aggression.[19]

As we have our origin in the creative power of love and are each of us born with the capacity to reflect that love, so we have a need to create lives and activities that mirror our inner reality. Yehudi Menuhin wrote in his autobiography of this essential human need and capacity to create:

> The creative, I firmly hold, is the normal human condition, whether displayed in the kitchen, in housekeeping, in violin-playing or in any of a hundred ways. That there is another definition of normality I am well aware, but I combat strenuously the view that equates the normal with that state of bodily and spiritual undernourishment in which most people have to live.[20]

Just as the frustration of purpose leads to depression, addiction and aggression, so too a condition of creative frustration will lead to vandalism, destruction and aggression.

> . . . the happiness and greatness, the rank and station, the pleasure and peace, of an individual have never consisted in his personal wealth, but rather in his excellent character, his high resolve, the breadth of his learning, and his ability to solve difficult problems.[21]

'The creative is the normal human condition'

A condition of creative frustration can lead to vandalism

Conclusion

To develop our two-fold capacity for loving and knowing –
this is what being a human is really about. This capacity does
not perish when our physical bodies perish but continues to
exist. A recent detailed study of the experiences of people who
have, physically, stopped living for some minutes during
major surgery reports a startling unanimity: those individuals
who have 'near-death-experiences' and are resuscitated return
to their normal lives with a deepened awareness of the
importance of love and knowledge in their lives.[22]

10

An Error Exposed

WE are part of the material creation and yet there is a spiritual dimension to human life which transcends the limitations of the animal world. At first sight this might lead us to imagine that these two aspects of ourselves must be in a continual tug-of-war. It is easy to imagine that in each one of us a battle rages between our primitive and perhaps 'instinctively aggressive' animal self and our higher spiritual self. It is this easy assumption – that there are two powerful forces battling it out, each trying to assert its ascendancy over the other – that lies behind our acceptance of the idea of our innate aggressiveness. But recent scientific research throws new light on our supposed strong instincts and provides us with a fresh and hopeful perspective. However, this inherited belief of instinctive human aggressiveness is so powerful and has held sway in different guises in human minds for so many centuries that it is not easy to dislodge. A first step must be to take a closer look at how it came into existence.

As we saw in the last chapter, we have a unique facility for spoken and written communication. As a result of this capacity, each of us, as a child, inherits a particular cultural tradition, a pattern of thought and a way of perceiving the world that affects all that we think and do. The vast majority of people living in Europe and North America share a common cultural heritage. While the west has no monopoly on war and violence in human history, western civilization is now, through the spread of its technology and values, affecting the lives of everyone living on earth. For this reason it is necessary to focus a little more closely on this particular inheritance of thought.

The roots of the theory

In Christian Europe during the Middle Ages there was an awareness of a strong and direct connection between the spiritual and material worlds. However, in the popular mind, the material creation itself was seen as fundamentally flawed and a source of evil to humankind. This was based, in large part, on a literal interpretation of the Judaic creation story as told in the Book of Genesis where the serpent and Eve together introduce sin into the Garden of Eden.

The discoveries of the scientific revolution shattered the mediaeval world view. While it was realized that the world was not at the centre of the universe, the traditional attitude towards the imperfection of the natural world continued but with a subtle change of emphasis. Western scientific man exulted in the power which his new knowledge and strength gave him over the environment, which he thought he could now subdue, dominate and exploit. In 1854 Chief Sealth observed the effects of the 'White Man's' new-found power.

> We know that the White Man does not understand our ways. One portion of land is the same to him as the next, for he is a stranger who comes in the night and takes from the land whatever he needs. The earth is not his brother, but his enemy, and when he has conquered it, he moves on . . .
> He treats his mother, the earth, and his brother, the sky, as things to be bought, plundered, sold like sheep or bright

beads. His appetite will devour the earth and leave behind only a desert.[1]

In the middle of the last century, when discoveries made by biologists and geologists established conclusively that the Biblical story of the creation could not be understood in a strictly literal sense, another variant of the inherited pattern of thought arose. Briefly, the thesis was that man is by instinct an aggressive creature and that his natural instinct for fighting both wild animals and other men accounts both for individual aggression and for the wars between nations. War was thus viewed as a primary factor in human evolution. It was, so the argument went, the need for the intellectual skills demanded by war that led to an increase in human brain size, that caused our early ancestors to fashion tools which they could use as weapons and to develop cooperative hunting and fighting skills that could be used not only against animals but against neighbouring 'aggressive hordes' of other humans.

This theory was revived and further developed in the 1950s and 1960s by a few widely-read and influential popular writers who combined this nineteenth-century theory with the results obtained from scientific research into the study of aggression in animals. The aggressive instinct in man, it was argued, is bound to dominate all human behaviour unless it is curbed and kept under control by laws and regulations. Furthermore, one best-selling author claimed, not only do we possess an 'ineradicable killer instinct' but we are also instinctively 'territorial creatures' supplied by our genes with a 'territorial imperative' which leads us to defend our territory against other humans.[2] Thus war and conflict are inevitable for they are programmed into our genes.

When one considers the massive slaughter and destruction of human life which has taken place since the middle of the last century, it is very understandable that this view of 'innate aggressiveness' has sunk deep into our minds. But this pessimistic view of human nature is challenged by scientists in many fields. As we shall see, there were, even from the outset, a number of serious flaws to the widely-accepted theory which have only gradually become evident.

Serious flaws

The idea that there is an innate aggressive element in human nature is based on a misunderstanding of the process of evolution itself. The phrase 'the survival of the fittest' has come to mean, in everyday language, the survival of the strongest or the survival of those able to make the most terrifying threats. But this is not the sense in which 'fittest' has been used by biologists from Darwin and Wallace onwards.

Being fit to survive does not necessarily mean physical strength at all, as Jane Beckman Lancaster, an anthropologist, explains. A selective advantage which enables one individual to adapt to its environment more successfully than another might be an extra dose of curiosity or adventurousness in obtaining food or an extra amount of care given by parents to their offspring.[3] The biologist Lewis Thomas puts it this way:

> The survival of the fittest does not mean those fit to kill; it means those fitting in best with the rest of life.[4]

When this is understood it can be seen that a tendency towards aggression in any organism, animal or human being would actually be selected *against* as it would constantly be putting the creature in which it developed into unnecessary danger.

Furthermore, in most animals aggression directed against members of the same species takes the form of displays or signals which induce intruders to withdraw and which seldom involve actual clashes. It is thus a social mechanism which throughout the animal kingdom ensures a hierarchical stability

within communities and which minimizes injuries which
could lead to death.

When the theory of evolution by natural selection was first
formulated considerable emphasis was placed on 'the struggle
for existence' that goes on in the natural world. It was this
struggle that greatly impressed Herbert Spencer, the first
person who applied it to the evolution of human society. But
in the present century, and particularly in recent decades,
much more attention is being paid by scientists to the many
instances of cooperation and interdependence that exist in the
natural world amongst plants and animals, both within and
between species.

Since this theory of human 'innate aggressiveness' was first
formulated, a great deal has been learnt by scientists about
instinct and aggression, both in animals and human beings.
Field research into the behaviour of both apes and monkeys
has shown that much of what was earlier assumed to be
instinctive behaviour in the higher primates is now known to
be learned. It is this fact which explains the long period of
infant dependency amongst the great apes. There is a great
deal that a young ape must learn if it is to live successfully
with its fellows. Even though the society is built on a pattern
of hierarchical dominance, which is of course entirely appropriate for animals, such communal living requires a good deal
of intelligence. Contrary to the popular assumption, it is living
in cooperative communities, whether animal or human, that
demands a high level of intelligence.

It is this fact which lies behind the remarkable capacity of
young chimpanzees and gorillas to learn American sign
language and to operate simple computer keyboards when
taught by humans. Their learning ability testifies to the
intelligence which is needed in the animals' lives in the wild.

The general picture that emerges from research into
aggression in animals is that the more complex the organism,

the less dependence there is on instinct and the greater necessity for learned behaviour. It is therefore perfectly logical, as well as being scientifically valid, that human beings, the most complex of all living organisms, are almost entirely instinctless. Ashley Montagu, a distinguished anthropologist and social biologist wrote in 1968:

> ... in spite of all attempts to saddle him with instincts, all such attempts have thus far failed ... there is not the slightest evidence or ground for assuming that the ... instinctive behaviour of other animals is in any way relevant to the discussion of the motive forces of human behaviour. The fact is that with the exception of the instinctoid reactions in infants to sudden withdrawals of support and to sudden loud noises, the human being is entirely instinctless ... man is man because he has no instincts, because everything he is and has become he has learned.[5]

It is difficult for many people to come to terms with the fact that we have no instincts. At first, such an idea seems completely contrary to common sense. There are several reasons for this widespread reaction. We often use the word 'instinct' loosely in everyday conversation without any awareness of its essential, scientific meaning. An instinct is, in scientific terms, a behaviour pattern which has three essential features. It is complex, it is unlearned and it appears in all normal members of the species under identical conditions.[6]

An instinct is therefore not the same thing as a simple muscular reflex. We all experience simple muscular reflexes when we start or jump at unexpectedly loud noises, when we touch something hot and quickly move our hand away or when we lose our balance and stretch our arms in order to regain it. In contrast to these simple reflexes, the complexity of instinctive behaviour can be seen in the nest building of birds. Every bird of the same species will carry out this complex, unlearned task in exactly the same way.[7]

We must also make a clear mental separation between instinctive behaviour patterns and the few basic organic urges that every human being experiences, for food, drink, warmth, shelter and sexual satisfaction. While these basic drives are common to all people, the way in which they are satisfied is learnt through cultural experience. Furthermore, human beings, unlike all other living creatures, have a unique capacity to override any or all of these drives completely, if they want to.[8]

If this theory of 'innate aggression' were sound, we could reasonably expect it to apply to all human beings on the planet. However, it is not universal either in our own society or in the rest of the world. Moreover, we have only recently realized that there are societies in the world, in the Arctic, in the Kalahari desert, in the equatorial forests of Africa, Asia and South America, where small, self-sufficient communities live cooperative and peaceful lives, albeit under threat from western 'civilization'.

Recent research by anthropologists into the lives and cultures of these communities has helped us to realize that the aggression we have thought of as natural and inevitable is a behavioural pattern. Where aggressive behaviour is rewarded it increases. When it is practised regularly, the tendency to act aggressively increases. Where it is not rewarded, it is hardly evident at all. One conclusion that might be drawn from this is that the more we watch violent films and videos, the more violence there will be in our societies.

There are almost no instincts at all programmed into our genes and certainly no aggressive ones. Instead, human beings have a highly developed capacity for learning and it is this capacity that many scientists, Ashley Montagu among them, regard as constituting our innate hominid nature.

Conclusion

Thus the idea which has held sway in Western thought for so many centuries of a conflict between body and mind in the form of a struggle between animal instincts and spiritual inclinations must be thoroughly revised in the light of new scientific knowledge. Particular attention must be paid to the human capacity for learning. We have learnt both to compete and to cooperate. Competition, whether in the form of a lethal arms race or in a contest for scarce planetary resources, would now appear to be an evolutionary dead-end. While we cannot deny that we have evolved through both competition and cooperation, we need to examine the role that cooperation has played in our past so that we can move forward confidently to a new level of cooperative endeavour. Such an exploration will enable us to recover a significant portion of our spiritual inheritance.

'We must', 'Abdu'l-Bahá stresses, 'strive unceasingly and without rest to accomplish the development of the spiritual nature in man, and endeavour with tireless energy to advance humanity toward the nobility of its true and intended station.'[9]

> There is a new reality, that man is a part of the cosmos and that, just as the individual cell needs the organism of which it is a part, mankind needs – and therefore cannot destroy – his world. Wisdom is becoming the new criterion of fitness.[10]

11

Discovering Our Past

THE discovery that we must revise our inherited assumptions about human nature leads to a second realization. We must also review the perspective we have of our own past, for it is now evident that this powerful inherited notion of our 'innate aggressiveness' has seriously distorted our view of our own history.

A fresh perspective

It is only very recently, as a result of discoveries made in the last three decades, that we have begun to gain some accuracy of perspective in viewing our human origins. From 1959 onwards, major fossil discoveries in Africa, and the systematic investigation of these fossils and the environments in which they were found, have enabled us to gain a view of our distant past which was unavailable to all earlier generations. The fossil discoveries reveal that between two and three million years ago there were groups of proto-humans or hominids living on the grassy plains of East Africa.

In 1976 Mary Leakey, working at Laetoli in Tanzania, discovered in a layer of ash a trail of fossilized footprints made by three hominids almost four million years ago. These, the oldest known footprints in the world were, Richard Leakey writes, 'unmistakably human and, very surprisingly, indistinguishable from footprints made by people today.'[1]

A detailed anatomical investigation of the most complete fossil of an early hominid yet discovered (by Donald Johanson in the Afar region of Ethiopia in 1974) – Lucy (*Australopithecus afarensis*) who lived over three million years ago – reveals that she too was an upright walker, although research into her pelvic structure suggests that her gait was probably more shambling than that of modern day humans.[2]

These recent discoveries are of particular significance, as Professor C. Owen Lovejoy explains:

> For most of this century evolutionary theorists have held that human ancestors evolved this strange mode of locomotion because it freed their hands to carry the tools their larger brains enabled them to make.[3]

From this assumption, it was but a step to state that human beings learnt to walk upright so that they could wield weapons with which to fight both wild animals and each other. Yet the research on Lucy's skeleton clearly establishes that:

> bipedality, with its many disadvantages, appeared long before our ancestors could have put their freed hands to use in carrying tools or weapons; it was part of a novel reproductive strategy that enabled the first hominids to flourish and diversify.[4]

Once the transition to upright walking was made, the early hominids gradually acquired the skills that led them to make tools, to live as gatherers, scavengers and hunters, and to develop a spoken language. This way of life, once established, continued for a very long time. It was only about thirty thousand years ago that people first began to herd animals. Later, only around ten thousand years ago, they first began to plant and reap their own crops. By twenty thousand years ago, the skulls and brains of our human ancestors were indistinguishable in size from our own. As Richard Leakey explains:

> To all intents and purposes the physical evolution of humans all over the world was complete by about twenty thousand years ago. We do not see any further major changes in the skulls, teeth and skeletons of human beings after that time. But what now begins to evolve rapidly are ideas, skills and ways of living.[5]

Correcting more errors

All this information has only come to light in this century and much of it only in recent decades. Thomas Hobbes, the influential philosopher who lived in the eighteenth century, of course knew nothing of these facts and could not possibly have had any idea of the immensely long and complex process of human evolution. He neatly disposed of the centuries and millennia of gathering-hunting life before there were formal laws and governments in a pithy and easily-memorized phrase: '. . . the life of man' was, Hobbes proposed, 'solitary, poor, nasty, brutish and short.'[6]

Hobbes' ideas, although not founded on scientific knowledge or observation, were, and still are, extremely influential. They certainly provided fertile ground in which the ideas of the Social Darwinists (those who believe that social and cultural advance is the product of competition and conflict between groups, with the socially elite possessing biological superiority in the struggle for existence) could take strong root, for Hobbes assumed that:

> During the time men live without a common power to keep them all in awe, they are in that condition which is called war. . . Whatsoever therefore is consequent to a time of

war, where every man is enemy to every man, the same is consequent to the time wherein men live without other security than what their own strength and their own invention shall furnish them withal . . .[7]

Partly from Hobbes and partly from the Social Darwinists we have inherited a traditional stereotyped image of our early ancestors. 'Man the hunter', we have been told, battled both against wild animals and neighbouring aggressive hordes while his children and female dependents cowered in the nearest cave awaiting his return from the fray.

Although it is certain that life was considerably shorter for most of our ancestors than it now is for some of us, the rest of the stereotype must be dismantled, for it does not fit the historical facts. New information on the human past, painstakingly gleaned by archaeologists and anthropologists, is now setting the record straight, enabling us to recover our true history and our authentic human heritage.

Since the study of archaeology began, scientists have had to rely on the evidence provided by fossilized remains of bones and the remnants of stone tools which are dug up to piece together a picture of early human life. But these same scientists have recently realized, after studying the lives of present-day gatherers and hunters, that the traditional studies of 'stones and bones' provide a distorted and one-sided view of early human history.

Gathering-hunting peoples such as the San, often miscalled Bushmen, of the Kalahari, rely just as much and sometimes more heavily on foods gathered by the women of the group than on meat brought home by the men. But the gathering sticks and collecting bags used by the women perish quickly. There is absolutely no trace in the fossil remains which archaeologists study of the bags and sticks that our ancient female ancestors undoubtedly used. However, the stone implements which it is commonly assumed were used for hunting or scavenging animals have survived and the bones of the actual animals can be found in fossil form. As Glyn Isaac, an archaeologist who worked in East Africa for many years explains:

> It is clear that as long as we do not correct for the imbalance created by the durability of bone as compared with that of plant residues, studies of human evolution will tend to have a male bias![8]

While so much has been made of the role of hunting in the human past, archaeologists are now attempting to find out how much food might have been obtained from hunting itself and how much from simple scavenging of animals already dead. Scavenging has none of the glamour of cooperative hunting but it may well have been equally life-sustaining to our distant ancestors. As the journal *New Scientist* reported in 1988:

> There is a growing belief among researchers that our distant ancestors combined scavenging with the hunting of small or medium-sized mammals, that these methods were complementary and that both strategies were essential to the survival of early peoples.[9]

From the over-emphasis placed on the role of men and hunting, a further distortion developed. It was assumed for many years that the skills developed in hunting were the primary factor in human evolution, in other words, human beings 'succeeded' because they were so good at killing, first animals and then each other. But recent researches also modify this assumption.

In the first place, the population density of early gathering–hunting groups was very low. The groups of people which existed at any time between two million and about thirty thousand years ago were so small that any hostilities either within these groups or between them and neighbouring groups would have endangered their very existence. Any serious reduction in numbers through the hostilities which are imagined would have made the maintenance of these small populations impossible. In other words, if there had been regular and widespread hostility between such groups, human beings would have soon wiped each other out and none of us would be alive today.[10] Thus the available evidence enables us to refute Thomas Hobbes' assumption that a state of war was the norm amongst our earliest ancestors. It suggests, on the contrary, that warfare was rare, an abnormality in behaviour, resorted to only in extremity.

Research into the lives of many present-day gathering–hunting peoples confirms these facts. Far from being tied to a particular area of land which they defend against all comers, these societies share overlapping, changeable territories. This openness and flexibility allows them easier access to food in times of drought and enables neighbouring groups to take advantage of local food shortages and surpluses. 'Everything points', Ashley Montagu explains, 'to the non-violence of the greater part of early man's life, to the contribution made by the increasing development of cooperative activities, the very social process of hunting itself, the invention of speech, the development of food-getting and food-preparing tools, and the like.'[11]

The role of women

While the emphasis has been placed, until very recently, exclusively on the role of men in making tools and in hunting and fighting, and while it was assumed that the males provided both food and protection for the more helpless females of the species, the role of women in early human history and the significant contributions they undoubtedly

made to the new evolutionary adaptations have been mini-
mized, if not totally ignored.

The use of tools for gathering food must have preceded their
use in hunting simply because the earliest hominids had not
developed the power and precision that are necessary for
hunting with tools. The small physical stature of the early
hominids and their very simple technology make it highly
improbable that they could have pursued, captured and killed
large, dangerous animals with tools. Female use of tools had
hardly a mention in the scientific literature until the 1980s, yet
Glyn Isaac and other archaeologists have uncovered very
ancient sites where 'scatterings of artifacts . . . sharp-edged
broken stones of the kind produced by deliberate percussion,
are often found without bone being present in significant
amounts.'[12]

In chimpanzee social groups it is the mothers that provide
the core of the most stable and long-lasting groups in the
communities. The bonds between mothers and their offspring
and the bonds between these related offspring are strong and
remain powerful throughout the lives of the individuals. It is,
in addition, the responsibility of the mothers first to provide
food for their offspring and then to teach the infants how to
fend for themselves.

Dr Nancy Makepeace Tanner, an anthropologist, draws
attention to the vital contribution to human evolution made
by the first 'gatherers of food', challenging us to reconsider the
role of the females of our ancestral species as they moved from
the forests to the grassy savanna country of East Africa.

Dr Tanner suggests, in the theoretical model she has
constructed of this crucial transitional period in our distant
past, that:

> Because of nutritional requirements of pregnancy and
> nursing and overt demands from hungry children, women
> had more motivation for technological inventiveness, for

Around ten thousand years ago we first began to plant and reap crops

It was only about thirty thousand years ago that people first began to herd animals

The bonds between mothers and their children are strong

creativity in dealing with the environment, for learning about plants and for developing tools to increase productivity and save time . . . Mothers who were the best gatherers – that is, who were most intelligent, who used tools most effectively, who walked and carried most efficiently and who shared gathered food – had children who were the most likely to survive. Among those surviving children, those best able to learn and improve on their mothers' techniques and those who, like their mothers were willing to share in turn, had the children who were most likely to live long enough to reproduce.[13]

The evolutionary strategy of cooperating to obtain and share food amongst the group is one we will explore in more detail in the next chapter.

Conclusion

These fresh insights and perspectives on human evolution can help us to rid ourselves of the distortions we have all inherited in thinking about the human past. An inaccurate knowledge of our own past history limits us and induces unnecessary cynicism and despair. Struggle and competition have undoubtedly played a part in making us what we are but the capacity to cooperate has, as we shall see in the next chapter, always been of greater importance to us.

12

Cooperation and Food-Sharing

RECENT research in several disciplines is enabling us to gain a more accurate picture of the vital part that cooperation has played in the evolution of human societies. At the same time, the work of biologists engaged in long-term field studies of the living great apes brings into sharp focus the behavioural differences that separate human beings from all other primates. When combined, the researches and discoveries of all these scientists enable us to identify certain patterns of individual and social behaviour that are uniquely human and that were already established amongst our hominid ancestors who lived between two and one million years ago.

The most interesting and significant difference in behaviour that exists between humans and all other primates can be found in the way that food is obtained and shared. As Jane Beckman Lancaster explains: 'The diet and food-getting behaviour of humans sets them off from other primates.'[1]

Chimpanzees and baboons do sometimes cooperate in the obtaining of food. Researchers have watched wild chimpanzees call others in their group to join them when they have found a tree with plenty of fruit. Other researchers have seen male baboons and chimpanzees cooperating in small groups when hunting small animals. Occasionally, a female chimpanzee has been seen bringing a handful of fruits to her aged mother who could not obtain them for herself. Meat is shared amongst chimpanzees but the sharing is more accurately described as 'tolerated scrounging' rather than active sharing.[2] Significant differences remain between the activities listed above and the way that humans both obtain food and actively share it with each other.

In the first place, the fossilized animal bones, together with the remains of simple stone tools and of ancient fires found at campsites dating back one and a half million years, reveal that a unique pattern of food-sharing was already established amongst our distant ancestors. As Glyn Isaac explains:

> Excavation of these proto-human sites has revealed evidence suggesting that two million years ago some elements that now distinguish men from apes were already part of a novel adaptive strategy. The indications are that a particularly important part of that strategy was food-sharing.[3]

Isaac identifies this uniquely hominid and later human behaviour in these words:

> Whereas humans may feed as they forage, just as apes do, apes do not regularly postpone food consumption until they have returned to a home base, as humans do.[4]

In other words, from very ancient times, while living a nomadic type of life, our distant ancestors began to carry to their temporary home bases some of the fruits of their foraging and hunting.

Secondly, the hominid ancestors of modern human beings very early on established a cooperative division of labour in food-gathering. The women went out with gathering sticks and bags and their small children to gather plant food – fruits, roots, nuts, seeds, plants, leaves – and small edible animals while the men cooperated in hunting or scavenging larger animals. This cooperative division of labour in food-gathering is not seen in any other primates. By collecting both plant and animal foods early hominids increased the diversity of their food sources and in this way made their lifestyles much more flexible. Jane Goodall reports that chimpanzees spend half their waking hours feeding and much of the rest of their time moving from one food source to the next. In contrast, modern-day gathering–hunting peoples spend only a few hours of each day in obtaining sufficient food for their families. By means of this evolutionary adaptation, our ancestors were freed from dependence on one particular type of food and environment. This freedom of mobility contributed to their ability to move into new areas in times of localized drought or shortages.

These unique human behavioural patterns which have been highlighted both by archaeology and primate research – the division of labour in obtaining food and the sharing of food at a group campsite – may well help to provide an answer to a question which has puzzled scientists for many decades. What was it that triggered such rapid evolutionary development in our remote ancestors? What was the key adaptive strategy that set human beings on the road to creating cultures and civilizations?

It was in an attempt to answer this very question that Herbert Spencer first put forward the idea of man's 'innate aggressiveness'. We were, Spencer and all his successors suggested, impelled to compete and to fight, and this provided our evolutionary imperative. But as we have seen, the work of scientists undertaken in this century shows that this theory is unsound. At the same time, the combined researches of archaeologists, biologists and anthropologists provide a base from which we may be able to find a genuine answer to this puzzle.

One fact emerges clearly from all the recent studies. Early proto-human hominids survived and flourished because they developed unique cooperative skills in searching for and sharing food. In 1979 Glyn Isaac presented as a working hypothesis the idea that this evolutionary adaptation of food-sharing was 'a behaviour central to a novel complex of adaptations that included as critical components hunting and/or scavenging, gathering and carrying.'[5]

It was this adaptive complex built around the active sharing of food, Isaac suggests, which enabled our hominid ancestors to make such rapid evolutionary progress. He explains that while certain behavioural patterns which later became important in human evolution, such as cooperation in the obtaining and sharing of food and the use of tools in obtaining food, can be observed in rudimentary form in chimpanzee groups, these behavioural patterns exist among chimpanzees in isolation from one another. But in early hominid societies the evidence suggests that a number of adaptations – the use of tools, the division of labour between men and women, the establishment of home bases, and the use of carrying equipment such as bags and containers – were brought together by the central adaptation of cooperating more actively to obtain and share food. Thus, each one of these separate adaptations, when connected by food-sharing, would have interacted with and strengthened all the others, reinforcing them all and speeding up evolutionary change.

Each one of these evolutionary adaptations would have contributed to the development of human language for it would have been necessary to describe accurately and agree on a place to meet and eat. This gathering to eat would, in its turn, have led to story-telling. We can even, with little effort, imagine the ancestor of all thwarted anglers recounting at an early campfire the saga of the biggest fish ever – the one that got away.

While hunting was only one of a number of cooperative skills developed by our early ancestors, it may well have been at the campfire that hunting first so captured and gained a hold on the human imagination. The quiet joys of gathering berries, nuts or mushrooms, and the sense of intimate communion with nature that such gathering provides, however satisfying for the individual involved, could in no way have compared with the drama and adventures of hunting as material with which to enliven the evening's story-telling.

At the same time, if we may judge from the traditional activities of present-day hunters in the Arctic, the Kalahari and elsewhere, from the reverent way in which they isolate and quickly despatch the one or two necessary animals, and from the apologies which they regularly make to the animals for the necessity of killing them in the first place, early men hunted not for the love of killing but in order to live, to provide food for their families and kin.

'Ferocity', 'Abdu'l-Bahá states emphatically, 'does not belong to the kingdom of man. It is the province of man to confer life, not death.'[6]

The cooperative division of labour must also have contributed significantly to the early evolution of human family life. Amongst our human ancestors, long-term mating bonds evolved that included reciprocal ties and joint obligations for aspects of child-rearing. It was this evolutionary adaptation that led to the formation of complex webs of kinship bonds that still link together gathering–hunting societies.

Care of the weak

There is at present a widespread view that it is only with the establishment of modern 'welfare states' that human beings have begun to take special care of individuals with disabilities that limit their activities; in 'primitive societies', we state glibly, 'the weakest have always gone to the wall.' But this assumption must also be revised in the light of new evidence.

Investigation of burials in Europe dating from Neanderthal times – approximately one hundred thousand to forty thousand years ago – have revealed that the Neanderthal people cared for the sick and elderly amongst them. The first relatively complete Neanderthal burial ever found, in France in 1908, was of an old man who suffered severely from arthritis, a slowly-developing and often incapacitating disease. This evidence of care for the elderly and sick is more remarkable when we realize that although the Neanderthals first appeared during a mild spell between ice ages in Europe, the last ice age began about seventy thousand years ago and lasted until about twelve thousand years ago.

After about thirty-five thousand years ago no further traces of Neanderthal peoples have been found. For about a hundred years, from the mid-nineteenth century onwards, when the first Neanderthal skeletons were found, it was thought that this absence of Neanderthal remains meant that they had been slaughtered by an incoming 'aggressive horde' of Cro-Magnon peoples. But skulls found in recent decades reveal a blend of Neanderthal and Cro-Magnon features, and scientists now have reason to believe that the Neanderthals gradually integrated peacefully with the Cro-Magnons, intermarrying with the newcomers and learning from them new skills. Once again, the inherited notion of ancient aggression must be set aside.

Moving closer to our own times – a mere eleven thousand years ago, in the stone age – a striking item of evidence has recently been dug up. In 1987 a group of scientists reported the discovery of an unusual skeleton in a cave in southern Italy. They had found the remains of a young man, buried in Upper Paleolithic times, who had suffered from birth from a severe growth deficiency. It is the earliest known case of dwarfism in the human record.

The shortness of stature and the immobility of elbow joints

which this deficiency caused would not only have made this young man profoundly different in appearance from the rest of his family and group but must have interfered greatly with his participation in the life of his community. He could not have hunted with the other men, and even keeping up with a nomadic group must have been a major problem in the rugged mountains where his people lived. Yet this youth was buried in a cave which is known to have been an important ritual centre where only a limited number of people of high rank or status were buried. This burial is silent but eloquent testimony to the fact that these early people both cared for and respected an individual who had more than one severe physical handicap and who had an extremly limited ability to contribute to their subsistence activities at a time when much of Europe was still uninhabitable and icy cold.[7]

Conclusion

Without the uniquely human cooperative skills developed in both obtaining and sharing food and in taking care of all members of a group, human social life would be little different from that of animals.

In the 1960s, U Thant, who was then Secretary-General of the United Nations, made an impassioned plea for co-operation in our world:

> . . . every sphere of activity of which man can declare himself to be proud and every achievement which he can claim to his credit has been the result of his willingness to subordinate his own narrow, selfish interests to the larger good, in other words, of his willingness to cooperate with others . . . every step forward on the highway of history has been the result of cooperation . . . cooperation is not only a natural condition of human progress but the pre-condition of continued human existence itself.[8]

While the threat of present-day world crises were undoubtedly uppermost in his mind, it is interesting to realize that his words are just as relevant to the lives of our distant ancestors as they are to our own.

Man, 'Abdu'l-Bahá writes, 'is in need of continuous cooperation and mutual help.'9 '. . . all progress is the result of association and cooperation . . .'10

II

BUILDING A NEW WORLD

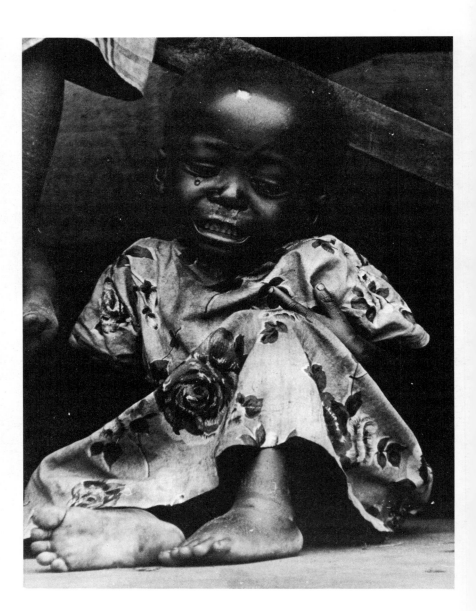

13

The Cause of the Present Crisis

IF we have no aggressive instincts programmed into our genes, if we are indeed sociable and cooperative creatures, why are we in our present mess? Why do three-quarters of the world's nations presently spend more on means of dealing death to each other than they do on preserving and nurturing life?

Why is it that we can deliver war-heads to cities on distant continents more quickly than we can get commuters to work in their own cities?

Why are vast numbers of the world's peoples either starving or malnourished while a small minority live in affluence?

Why are we so thoughtlessly destroying the fragile eco-system on which our very existence depends?

What happened? What went wrong?

We have already seen that the various urgent crises the world faces are inextricably linked to each other and that we cannot solve any one in isolation from the others. This is becoming daily more evident. As the World Commission on Environment and Development reported in 1987: 'These are not separate crises: an environmental crisis, a development crisis, an energy crisis. They are all one.'[1]

We also have learnt that the interlocked global crises of

militarism, poverty, ecology and development are in essence ethical problems, that is, that they arise from the way we regard the world and each other.

'The reality of man', 'Abdu'l-Bahá wrote, 'is his thought, not his material body.'[3]

Everything that we do, behavioural scientists inform us, is the result of what we think; all our actions, both individual and collective, are the outcome and product of our values, convictions, attitudes and beliefs.

The eminent philosopher and peace campaigner Bertrand Russell, writing of the causes of warfare, explained that, 'The trouble lies in the minds of men . . . it is in enlightening the minds of men that the cure must be sought.'[3]

Albert Einstein, a thinker many decades ahead of his contemporaries, repeatedly warned of the urgent and desperate need for a new way of thinking in a nuclear world: 'The unleashed might of the atom', he wrote, 'has changed everything except our thinking. We are consequently moving toward an unparalleled disaster. We shall need a substantially new way of thinking if mankind is to survive.'[4]

A realization that we must change our attitudes and our values before we can change our behaviour is now spreading rapidly amongst people all over the world. But having reached this realization, many people throw up their hands in panic and despair. 'Where are we to find such a new way of thinking? How can we possibly change?' they ask. 'It's already too late and the problems are getting worse every day. It's all just too difficult!'

We have to go one step further in our understanding of the problem and realize that the crises we are now encountering are interrelated aspects of a universal spiritual crisis. Over fifty years ago, when the disease was already well-established, Shoghi Effendi explained that 'the universal crisis affecting mankind is . . . essentially spiritual in its causes.'[5]

The problems which now threaten our common future are symptoms of a deep spiritual sickness which exists at the very root of human life in every country and every continent of the globe. The crisis has come about because we have failed to give adequate attention to vital spiritual guidance made available to us over a hundred years ago in the life and the writings of Bahá'u'lláh.

Bahá'u'lláh brought to humanity all the guidance we need to pass safely from the turbulence of our collective adolescence into the beginning of maturity. But adolescents seldom either listen to or act on advice; they prefer to find things out their own way, through painful experience. So it has been at the culminating point in the collective adolescence of humanity. It is because we have not heeded or acted upon the guidance contained in the Bahá'í Revelation that we see about us not merely signs of change and growth but symptoms of serious and life-threatening disease.

But it is not too late. The first seeds of spiritual change and growth were sown on our planet over a hundred years ago. They have taken root and the mystic but all-pervasive passage from adolescence to maturity is already occurring. The process of spiritual change, of a renewal of our innermost thoughts and attitudes, is now well under way. As 'Abdu'l-Bahá explains:

> When a divine spiritual illumination becomes manifest in the world of humanity, when divine instruction and guidance appear, then enlightenment follows, a new spirit is realized within, a new power descends, and a new life is given.[6]

14

The Essential Connection

THE life of all living things, the germination of a seed or the early development of an embryo, begins in darkness and apparent invisibility. The beginning of a spiritual revival in the life of humanity also begins in darkness and initial obscurity. As the shoot of a young plant pushes its way upwards, breaking through a crust of covering soil to stretch and unfold in light and air, so too the infant shoot of a new revelation from God to humankind must break through a crust of inherited thought, tradition and belief before human beings can rise to new levels of accomplishment.

The seed is not left to struggle alone; the light and warmth of the sun and the showers of rain call it out of the earth. Nor are we left alone to struggle with our singular and tremendous endowment of spiritual and intellectual capacity. A just and loving Creator who has provided for all the material needs of His creatures has also provided for the training and development of the souls of men and women. But we have to do our own part in growing; we must stretch our own limbs and use our own minds. We cannot move into a secure, happy and productive maturity until we change and grow in our innermost selves, until we venture to explore new, mature and responsible pathways of thought. Only then will we be able to move on from the attitudes and actions of adolescence which presently confine us and limit our possibilities.

Nowhere is the need for such a change of thought more striking than in the area of religion, for religious prejudices are a powerful cause of alienation, division, discrimination and war. So many irreligious actions have been carried out in the name of religion that the very mention of the word throws up an automatic barrier in many people's minds. When religion has itself become part of the problem, few people imagine that it might have anything to offer to the solution of the present crises.

A fresh perspective

As children we live almost entirely in the present or in the immediate future. We are so busy experiencing and exploring the world about us that we have little time or need to think about the past. It is only as adolescents that we begin to look back on memorable events in our childhood and only as we begin to approach maturity that we become able to see the shape and pattern of our own childhood and begin to understand the significance it has for our adult life. As children grow taller they gain a wider view of their physical environment; as we stand on the brink of our collective maturity we are now able to see and understand much that we could not see or understand as children.

'The Revelation,' Bahá'u'lláh states emphatically, 'of which I am the bearer is adapted to humanity's spiritual receptiveness and capacity.'[1]

The Bahá'í teachings offer a fresh perspective on religion which is suited to our emerging maturity. They provide an insight into the nature of religion and its development which enables people from all backgrounds to overcome traditional prejudices, to gain a deeper insight into their own particular inheritance and to discover the relevance and significance of other religious systems.

How do we learn?

At a physical level, we inhabit a world of strict physical limitations. Every living thing around us, all plants and animals, come into being, flourish and then die. Our own bodies participate in this endless physical cycle. Where, in such a world, did we ever get the idea that there is anything immortal? How did we come to realize that there are such things as justice, goodness and truth? Did we arrive at these ideas by ourselves? Are they the result of our own unaided human thought and imagination? Did it happen because human beings have some sort of natural sense of honour and dignity?

The Bahá'í writings state that we did not formulate such ideas on our own; indeed we could never have done so, for as 'Abdu'l-Bahá explains:

The spirit of man is not illumined and quickened through material sources. It is not resuscitated by investigating phenomena of the world of matter.[2]

Without training and guidance the soul could never progress beyond the conditions of its lower nature, which is ignorant and defective.[3]

Without spiritual teachers to train and develop our souls we would be in the pathetic and tragic situation of children without parents or any other adults to feed, clothe and guide them. A child that is not trained to think of and care for others will remain forever imprisoned within its own selfishness and its undesirable qualities will strengthen from day to day. Left to itself, it cannot attain to any sense of human honour or dignity.

The Messengers of God

All that we need for the training of our spiritual reality comes to us through a series of divine spiritual teachers. In the Bahá'í writings these teachers of humanity are sometimes referred to as 'Messengers', as they bring guidance from God to humanity, or at other times as 'Manifestations', because they manifest the light of divine guidance in the human world. They have founded the religions of the world. They came in darkness and obscurity. They were opposed, mocked, scorned and bitterly persecuted but, alone and unaided by any earthly power, They changed the condition of the world in which They appeared and made new growth and development possible for humanity. They are, as 'Abdu'l-Bahá explains:

> . . . the divine Gardeners Who till the earth of human hearts and minds . . . The wisdom and purpose of Their training is that man must pass from degree to degree of progressive unfoldment until perfection is attained.[4]

We will never know when the first Messenger of God appeared on earth but Bahá'u'lláh explains that from the earliest, most remote times, all that was needed for the training of humanity was brought by a series of divine teachers. 'There have been', 'Abdu'l-Bahá states, 'many holy manifestations of God. One thousand years ago, two hundred thousand years ago, one million years ago, the bounty of God was flowing, the radiance of God was shining, the dominion of God was existing.'[5]

As They all bring down the light of divine guidance into the world, They all shine with the same light: 'Every one of them is the Way of God that connecteth this world with the realms above . . . They are the Manifestations of God amidst men, the evidences of His Truth, and the signs of His glory.'[6]

Their appearances are successive and correlated and their

purpose is one and the same – 'to bring this young child, humanity, to the stage of adulthood'.[7]

A two-fold station

The divine Messengers have a two-fold station. They are, in their physical bodies, like all other humans. They are born, they know joy and sorrow, they feel hunger and pain, they experience human life as other human beings do. However, their spiritual reality is infinitely different from and far greater than that of any other human being. Bahá'u'lláh describes their spiritual station in these words:

> These sanctified Mirrors, these Day Springs of ancient glory, are, one and all, the Exponents on earth of Him Who is the central Orb of the universe, its Essence and ultimate purpose. From Him proceed their knowledge and power, from Him is derived their sovereignty . . . Through them is transmitted a grace that is infinite, and by them is revealed the Light that can never fade.[8]

A two-fold purpose

A growing infant or child is in constant need of love, security, warmth, food and guidance, but its specific needs vary according to its age. The food, clothes, daily routine and activities of a toddler differ markedly from those of a ten-year-old but the individual is the same person, whether he or she be two or ten.

Humanity's need of spiritual guidance is constant but the specific needs of different times and ages vary.

'Every age', Bahá'u'lláh explains, 'requireth a fresh measure of the light of God. Every Divine Revelation hath been sent down in a manner that befitted the circumstances of the age in which it hath appeared.'[9]

Every religion has, therefore, two distinct but complementary aspects, an inner spiritual aspect and an outer, material form. 'Religion', 'Abdu'l-Bahá states, 'is the outer expression of the divine reality.'[10]

The Messengers of God awaken and develop the human capacity for loving and knowing. They all teach that there is a higher law for us than mere physical survival and that the honour and distinction of man is in service and humility. They teach us to treat others as we ourselves wish to be treated. They show us how to overcome fear and to have hope for the future. They never compel but they create in us the will to act, the desire to follow their own examples.

The Messengers of God come not only to lighten our inner spiritual condition but to improve the condition of the world in which They appear. Because the needs and capacities of human beings have evolved and differed, just as children's do even in the same family, the outward aspects of their teaching vary from age to age and from place to place. But the material aspects of religion – the laws, the customs and the social institutions which come into being after the appearance of a Messenger of God – are not eternal. They will be altered and renewed at the coming of a new Messenger of God to meet the needs of an evolving humanity.

'The religion of God is one,' 'Abdu'l-Bahá explains, 'and it is the educator of humankind, but still, it needs must be made new'.[11]

> The world of the Kingdom is one world. The only difference is that spring returneth over and over again, and setteth up a great new commotion throughout all created things. Then plain and hillside come alive, and trees turn delicately green, and leaves, blossoms and fruits come forth in beauty, infinite and tender. Wherefore the dispensations of past ages are intimately connected with those that follow them: indeed, they are one and the same, but as the world groweth, so doth the light, so doth the downpour of heavenly grace . . .[12]

15

Coming of Age

WE are used to thinking of individuals coming of age, but the idea of the whole of humanity coming of age is new and somewhat strange. As it is something that has never happened before in the history of the world, many people are understandably puzzled or sceptical and some dismiss the idea out of hand as impossible or absurd.

Responsible parents do all that they can to guide their children through the turbulence of adolescence and help them to anticipate and prepare for their own maturity. Bahá'u'lláh, who has come for the specific purpose of enabling us to achieve our collective maturity, explains to us what our coming of age will consist of and assures us that it is now within our reach. His teachings enable us to look beyond the present turmoil of world affairs and gain a vision of the possibilities of our future.

'The onrushing winds of the grace of God', He writes, 'have passed over all things. Every creature hath been endowed with all the potentialities it can carry . . . Every tree hath been endowed with the choicest fruits, every ocean enriched with the most luminous gems. Man, himself, hath been invested with the gifts of understanding and knowledge.'[1]

As explained in the Introduction, the coming of age of

humanity involves the achievement of the organic and spiritual unity of all the world's peoples and nations. It is a process that has already begun but because the kings and rulers of the world, both secular and religious, refused the guidance offered to them by Bahá'u'lláh, our progress towards it is slow and painful. It will be reached in two stages. Before the end of this century, the hostile and warring governments of the world will cooperate together in a political armistice. Bahá'u'lláh refers to this preparatory stage in the movement towards world peace as the 'Lesser Peace'.

Secondly, and over a longer period of time, a stage of universal justice and harmony will gradually be achieved. This latter stage of unity Bahá'u'lláh calls the 'Most Great Peace'. When it is finally achieved, when we can see and experience a world that is 'organically unified in all the essential aspects of its life, its political machinery, its spiritual aspiration, its trade and finance, its script and language, and yet infinite in the diversity of the national characteristics of its federated units'[2] – then we shall know that humanity has achieved its coming of age. Then all the possibilities of maturity will lie ahead of us.

The achievement of our organic and spiritual unity will mark, Shoghi Effendi explains,

> the last and highest stage in the stupendous evolution of man's collective life on this planet. The emergence of a world community, the consciousness of world citizenship, the founding of a world civilization and culture . . . should, by their very nature, be regarded, as far as this planetary life is concerned, as the furthermost limits in the organization of human society, though man, as an individual, will, nay must indeed as a result of such a consummation, continue indefinitely to progress and develop.[3]

This vision of the future is mind-stretching, and in order to understand it better we need to explore it from a number of aspects.

Preparation for maturity

In the life of an individual all the various stages of early life through which each of us must pass – the nine months of gestation, the longer periods of infancy, childhood and youth – are all essential stages of preparation for maturity.

The characteristic features of maturity are a calmness of mind, a depth of knowledge and wisdom which can enable people to make mature choices, decisions and judgements, an ability to appreciate the views of others and to have consideration for their needs and rights. But these qualities are not arrived at easily and they are only reached through individual struggle and by painful trial and error. It is an undeniable fact that we all – children, youth and adults – learn more from our painful mistakes than from our easy successes. People go on learning all their lives and there is no adult who never makes a mistake, but as youth we are bound to make them, for they are a very necessary part of finding out who we are and what our purpose is. We are eager for life and sometimes we rush into action without any thought for its consequences. But gradually we learn to act responsibly, to manage our resources, to plan for the future and to focus our energies on activities that will help us to develop our inner potential.

The long, painstaking preparation for the initiation into our collective maturity has been going on as long as there have been human beings on the planet. Every previous Messenger of God has helped us forward towards it. There have been many mistakes, cruelties and tragedies in the collective life of humanity, for human beings learn their spiritual lessons slowly and are prone to error. But we do not judge adults by the mistakes that they make in their childhood and youth. In the same way, we must beware of the danger, while we toss in the present troughs of anguish and despair, of condemning ourselves on our past record. The Universal House of Justice explains that:

> A candid acknowledgement that prejudice, war and exploitation have been the expression of immature stages in a vast historical process and that the human race is today experiencing the unavoidable tumult which marks its collective coming of age is not a reason for despair but a prerequisite to undertaking the stupendous enterprise of building a peaceful world.[4]

The means of unity

In the life of an individual the development of physical maturity precedes the achievement of spiritual, intellectual, emotional and social maturity. Our physical maturity is something that simply happens to us but all the other aspects of maturity must be striven for and require effort on our part. We can find a parallel situation in the history of the world. The physical means of our collective maturity already exist; they are the result of centuries of individual effort, of ever-widening knowledge and increasingly sophisticated technology but they have shown themselves in a recent and very rapid spurt of growth. As 'Abdu'l-Bahá explained in the early years of this century:

> In cycles gone by, though harmony was established, yet, owing to the absence of means, the unity of all mankind could not have been achieved. Continents remained widely divided, nay even among the peoples of one and the same continent association and intercourse of thought were well nigh impossible. Consequently intercourse, understanding and unity amongst all the peoples and kindreds of the earth

were unattainable. In this day, however, means of communication have multiplied, and the five continents of the earth have virtually merged into one. . . In like manner all the members of the human family, whether peoples or governments, cities or villages, have become increasingly interdependent. For none is self-sufficiency any longer possible, inasmuch as political ties unite all peoples and nations, and the bonds of trade and industry, of agriculture and education, are being strengthened every day. Hence the unity of all mankind can in this day be achieved.[5]

The necessary physical preparation is all in place but most of the essential spiritual, intellectual, emotional and social adjustments still lie ahead of us. We are in a halfway house, a position neatly summarized by the United Nations Commission on the Environment and Development: 'The earth is one but the world is not.'[6]

Experts of all kinds have, for the last forty years or more, written countless documents stressing the urgent need for the world's peoples to cooperate. But we continue to find it very difficult to do so because we cling to obsolete, adolescent patterns of thought and behaviour.

'Abdu'l-Bahá explains:

That which was applicable to human needs during the early history of the race can neither meet nor satisfy the demands of this day, this period of newness and consummation. Humanity has emerged from its former state of limitation and preliminary training. Man must now become imbued with new virtues and powers, new moral standards, new capacities. New bounties, perfect bestowals, are awaiting and already descending upon him. The gifts and blessings of the period of youth, although timely and sufficient during the adolescence of mankind, are now incapable of meeting the requirements of its maturity.[7]

16

The Key to Peace

A human being is part of the whole, called by us the universe. A part limited in time and space. He experiences himself, his thoughts and feelings, as something separate from the rest, a kind of optical delusion of his consciousness. This delusion is a kind of prison for us, restricting us to our personal desires and to affection for a few persons nearest to us. Our task must be to free ourselves from this prison by widening our circle of compassion to embrace all living creatures.[1]

WHEN a Messenger of God appears on earth, He releases new potential and capacity in human souls and these emerging capacities enable peoples and nations to progress both spiritually and materially. Bahá'u'lláh, the latest of God's Messengers, has released a new capacity in every human soul and He has bestowed on each one of us a gift exactly suited to our evolving capacity and our urgent needs. It is this gift which will enable us to acquire the qualities and characteristics of maturity: 'The gift of God to this enlightened age', 'Abdu'l-Bahá states, 'is the knowledge of the oneness of mankind and of the fundamental oneness of religion.'[2]

The Bahá'í concept of oneness and of unity can be difficult to grasp at first because we are hampered by our own limited

thoughts. We tend to think of oneness as a dull sameness and
to confuse unity with uniformity. We need to enlarge our own
understanding of the concept of unity and then apply this new
understanding to the world about us.

An exploration of unity

In the material world, unity is that which causes life for it is
through the joining together of different elements that all
forms of life, whether mineral, vegetable or animal, are able to
come into being. 'Abdu'l-Bahá writes:

> Look about thee at the world: here unity, mutual attraction,
> gathering together, engender life, but disunity and inhar-
> mony spell death. When thou dost consider all phenomena,
> thou wilt see that every created thing hath come into being
> through the mingling of many elements, and once this
> collectivity of elements is dissolved, and this harmony of
> components is dissevered, the life form is wiped out.[3]

In the natural world it is the diversity of the many elements
mingling together which provides the rich basis for the
development of new life forms. Diversity in natural systems is
a source of strength; it provides a key for successful adaptation
and evolution.

At the human level the same principle can be observed.
From the cooperation of men and women to raise their
children, a new institution, the human family, was born.
When all family members are able to develop their particular
skills and talents and contribute them freely for the welfare of
all, families flourish.

'If love and agreement are manifest in a single family',
'Abdu'l-Bahá explains,

> that family will advance, become illumined and spiritual;
> but if enmity and hatred exist within it, destruction and

dispersion are inevitable. This is, likewise, true of a city. If those who dwell within it manifest a spirit of accord and fellowship it will progress steadily and human conditions will become brighter . . . In the same way, the people of a nation develop and advance toward civilization and enlightenment through love and accord and are disintegrated by war and strife. Finally, this is true of humanity itself in the aggregate.[4]

We may think of the unity towards which the world is moving as the unity which links together the limbs, organs and faculties of an individual human body. Each limb or organ is specific and distinct but all are created to function harmoniously together, each has a vital role to contribute to the functioning of the whole organism. When one part of the body is prevented from functioning properly, the whole body suffers the consequences.

While we in the western world remain in our adolescent and spiritually diseased condition, some parts of the world body are starved of essential nutrients and others are heavily overweight. Even after the dramatic changes of the past few years, still more than half the body's energy and resources is consumed in the production of weapons posed for instant deployment, many of which pose a fatal threat to the whole organism. All members of the body are still struggling to go their own way, many without regard for the rights of other members and without any thought for the consequences of their actions. The body of the world remains at war with itself and the result is a condition of exhausting paralysis. Early this century 'Abdu'l-Bahá wrote:

> The world is even as a human being who is diseased and impotent, whose eyes can see no longer, whose ears have gone deaf, all of whose powers are corroded and used up.[5]

It is only a new awareness of our essential 'oneness and

wholeness', a knowledge which consists both of scientific facts and spiritual consciousness, that can help us out of this distressing condition.

Scientific knowledge of our unity

As we have seen, the roots of maturity in the life of every individual stretch far back into childhood but it is only in the stress of adolescence that the signs of maturity begin to appear. The roots of our collective maturity also stretch very far back but it is only now, during the turbulence of our collective adolescence, that the signs and evidences of our emerging maturity are beginning to appear. Only in this present century have we come to a scientific realization of the unity of the human species and of its utter dependence on its physical environment, a knowledge which has existed in many cultures at an intuitive level for centuries:

> This we know. The earth does not belong to man: man belongs to the earth. This we know. All things are connected like the blood which unites one family. All things are connected. Whatever befalls the earth befalls the sons of earth. Man did not weave the web of life, he is merely a strand in it. Whatever he does to the web, he does to himself.[6]

Only now can this knowledge be scientifically proven and demonstrated.

There is only one human species; all the human sciences now affirm this fact. At the very beginning of this century research into the composition of human blood revealed that the same basic pattern of blood structure and composition exists in people all over the world. More recently research in anthropology and archaeology reveals that we are indeed one human family with a common place of origin, probably somewhere in sub-Saharan Africa.

This knowledge of our origins, together with the recent researches of biologists and anthropologists, enable us to understand why we now look physically different from one another and why our cultures and traditions differ so sharply. For the first time in human history we can come to a scientific understanding of the diversity of the human family.

We saw in an earlier chapter that our distant ancestors developed cooperative skills that enabled them to migrate to new areas. As they moved into colder climates their bodies adapted to cope with the climatic changes. As they moved north from Africa, their skins became paler so that they could use the meagre available sunlight to manufacture vitamin D, an essential ingredient in skeletal formation; people moving north developed longer nasal passages than their southern cousins so that they could warm up the chilly air they had to breathe before it entered their lungs, and so on.

We also saw that human beings are born without instincts. As peoples separated from one another and as many groups became isolated from other human beings, they developed many different ways of living, different languages and different customs.

In addition to the knowledge gained about human beings, we have, in recent decades, come to a new awareness of the interdependence of all forms of life on our planetary home. This knowledge is also the fruit of centuries of earlier work but only now are the facts clearly emerging. As a result of the age-long, gradual extension of human knowledge, all the sciences reveal to us what seers and poets and many indigenous peoples have known for centuries: that the earth is, in reality, a single, highly-complex, living, breathing organism. We are now able to understand that we live 'in a house of unimaginable intricacy'[7] with which we meddle at our peril.

Most dramatically and unexpectedly, we have seen a new view of our home. It is already recognized by many leading thinkers and by ordinary people the world over that the most significant and lasting legacy of the space flights is the fresh perspective they have given us of our own planet.

> Once a photograph of the earth, taken from the outside is available . . . a new idea as powerful as any in history, will let loose.[8]

Suddenly we see our home from the outside. There are no barriers and no boundaries visible, only a small, solitary globe, beautiful, fragile and undeniably one.

'Man can withstand anything', 'Abdu'l-Bahá writes, 'except that which is divinely intended and indicated for the age and its requirements.'[9]

But with all this knowledge at our command we remain paralyzed and hampered by prejudices, doubts and misconceptions of all kinds. In the 1980s military spending tripled until the world spent more than $900,000,000,000 annually on armaments. There are now four and half thousand plants and animals at imminent risk of extinction. Several species become extinct every day; if things do not change, in ten years time it will be several every hour. If the present rate of tropical deforestation – an acre a second – continues unchecked, the once-vast Amazon forest will disappear by the end of the century and in only a few decades there will be no tropical forests left anywhere on this planet. Today there is less than two per cent of the world's dry tropical forest left. There are now more refugees and more hungry and impoverished people alive today than there were ten years ago. Wherever industrial emissions are produced and automobiles exist, acid rain is devastating forests and killing lakes and streams. In addition, all these critical problems are now compounded by the very real threat of global warming.

Until we come to a spiritual change, to a new spiritual awareness of the oneness of the human family, we shall not be able to act effectively: 'one single matter cannot,' 'Abdu'l-Bahá writes,

> by itself influence the human reality . . . for until the minds of men become united, no important matter can be accomplished . . . universal Peace is a matter of great importance but unity of conscience is essential, so that the foundation of this matter may become secure, its establishment firm and its edifice strong.[10]

A spiritual awareness of unity

Many people now realize that patriotism and nationalism alone are not sufficient for our needs. We need a wider awareness of the human community and a sense of global loyalty that will enable us to transcend narrow and short-sighted self-interest. A change in consciousness has already begun. People are already working in innumerable ways to save the planet and its myriad living creatures from destruction and extinction. All this activity, all the networking, all the consciousness-raising, all the striving for new, peaceful ways of solving problems and for increasing cooperation and understanding amongst ordinary people, are expressions of a new spirit which is alive in the world. This new impulse towards unity was implanted in human consciousness by Bahá'u'lláh, by His long life of suffering and by the creative words which He revealed and through which He has 'breathed a new life into every human frame'.[11]

The purpose of every Messenger of God is to bring about a transformation in the character of the people amongst whom He appears. Bahá'u'lláh states emphatically that His teachings were never intended for only one land or one people: they are for every person on the planet. The transformation we are now going through as we adjust to an awareness of the oneness of humanity is an immense one with far-reaching consequences. Bahá'u'lláh writes of the change in these words:

> Through each and every one of the verses which the Pen of the Most High hath revealed, the doors of love and unity have been unlocked and flung open to the face of men. We have erewhile declared – and Our Word is the truth –: 'Consort with the followers of all religions in a spirit of friendliness and fellowship.' Whatsoever hath led the children of men to shun one another, and hath caused dissensions and divisions amongst them, hath, through the revelation of these words, been nullified and abolished. . . The highest essence and most perfect expression of whatsoever the peoples of old have either said or written hath, through this most potent Revelation, been sent down from the heaven of the Will of the All-Possessing, the Ever-Abiding God. Of old it hath been revealed: 'Love of one's country is an element of the Faith of God.' The Tongue of Grandeur hath, however, in the day of His manifestation proclaimed: 'It is not his to boast who loveth his country, but it is his who loveth the world.' Through the power released by these exalted words He hath lent a fresh impulse and set a new direction to the birds of men's hearts, and hath obliterated every trace of restriction and limitation from God's holy Book.[12]

'Abdu'l-Bahá explains the significance of the new impulse to unity in these words:

> O peoples of the world! The Sun of Truth hath risen to illumine the whole earth, and to spiritualize the community of man. Laudable are the results and the fruits thereof, abundant the holy evidences deriving from this grace. This is mercy unalloyed and purest bounty; it is light for the world and all its peoples; it is harmony and fellowship, and love and solidarity; indeed it is compassion and unity, and

'The diversity in the human family should be the cause of love and harmony'

the end of foreignness; it is the being at one in complete
dignity and freedom with all on earth.[13]

There are many evidences of this new awareness of the
spiritual oneness of all peoples. Indeed, one of the most
striking characteristics of our time is the unprecedented
number of international humanitarian organizations which
have sprung into being in recent decades and which are
devoted to the service of all humanity, regardless of creed,
colour or nationality. They are the shoots and tendrils of the
new spiritual springtime which is dawning in the hearts of
men and women everywhere. A new, creative and dynamic
power already exists in the world. As Shoghi Effendi explains:

. . . this transcending love [for all humanity] . . . is neither
mysterious nor can it be said to have been artificially
created. It is both spontaneous and genuine.[10]

The widening of our spiritual horizons, together with the
explanation that religious truth is revealed progressively, in
accordance with the needs of an evolving humanity, provides
a foundation on which people from all backgrounds can
achieve a new level of spiritual unity.

The directive to consort with the followers of all religions is
far removed from a passive tolerance, it is very different from
merely enduring or suffering others. It entails a positive
awareness of the riches and benefits to be gained from human
diversity, an appreciation that 'the Glory of Humanity is the
heritage of each one'.[15]

'Abdu'l-Bahá writes:

Behold a beautiful garden full of flowers, shrubs, and trees.
Each flower has a different charm, a peculiar beauty, its
own delicious perfume and beautiful colour . . . The garden
which is pleasing to the eye and which makes the heart
glad, is the garden in which are growing side by side flowers
of every hue, form and perfume, and the joyous contrast of

colour is what makes for charm and beauty... The diversity in the human family should be the cause of love and harmony, as it is in music where many different notes blend together in the making of a perfect chord.[16]

This new awareness of the value of diversity leads to a respect for the achievements of others and to a willingness to learn from others. 'All men', Bahá'u'lláh writes, 'have been created to carry forward an ever-advancing civilization.'[17] Every people has some talent or insight to contribute, not only those who have developed western science and technology. We need to develop the humility that will enable us to learn from the people who can live in harmony with their environment without destroying it. We need intuitive wisdom as well as scientific knowledge and technology. We need to develop the feminine qualities of compassion and caring, of reverence and respect for all life which have been repressed for centuries by a technological civilization obsessed with power and the amassing of material wealth.

'Bahá'u'lláh has drawn the circle of unity', 'Abdu'l-Bahá writes,

> he has made a design for the uniting of all the peoples, and for the gathering of them all under the shelter of the tent of universal unity. This is the work of the Divine Bounty, and we must all strive with heart and soul until we have the reality of unity in our midst, and as we work, so will strength be given unto us.[18]

It is unity that will lead us to peace. In the life of an individual it is only a knowledge of the spiritual and material dimensions of our lives that can help us towards meaningful and fruitful lives. In world affairs the knowledge of the essential oneness and wholeness of humanity at both a spiritual and scientific level is the only foundation on which we can build a just and peaceful world.

17

Essential Building-Blocks

As we saw earlier, peace and harmony within an individual are the result of a person's awareness of his or her spiritual reality and can be achieved only when one strives to build on this awareness. Bahá'u'lláh has come to regenerate the spiritual life of every individual, to revive and refresh disappointed hearts and shattered hopes and to renew the virtues of honesty and integrity which are the foundation of all progress.

The next stage in the process of peace-building is the establishment of peace between individuals. This must be an organic development from the core of the individual into the world. But personal saintliness alone will not bring peace in today's world. There is a need for transformation at all levels of society if there is to be justice in the world. The theories and dogmas on which the present power structures are built are, for the most part, based on concepts of struggle and conflict and on long-established patterns of exploitation. As the oneness and interdependence of all the world's peoples is the new reality of our age, all these dogmas and systems of earlier ages are totally inadequate for our needs.

'Old ideas and modes of thought', 'Abdu'l-Bahá writes, 'are fast becoming obsolete. Ancient laws and archaic ethical systems will not meet the requirements of modern conditions. . .'[1]

While a prisoner and exile, Bahá'u'lláh outlined a number of principles which He knew that humanity would have need of in this critical transitional period of growth from youth to maturity. While individuals and societies have striven for some of them in recent centuries, their interdependence had never, before the coming of Bahá'u'lláh, been stressed nor had they been woven firmly into one dynamic and coherent whole. They are the essential building-blocks of justice and the only secure foundation on which we can build a peaceful world. Because the process of growth is an organic one we can find them emerging, slowly, through the present turmoil and confusion in world affairs. They are evidences of our emerging maturity and they are already at work, like yeast in the dough of our world. A few are now widely accepted, others are not yet seen as necessary or even desirable and none are as yet fully implemented in the world. But, as 'Abdu'l-Bahá explains:

> Unless these Teachings are effectively spread among the people, until the old ways, the old concepts, are gone and forgotten, this world of being will find no peace. . .[2]

As we know that all the current world crises are closely interconnected and that none of them can be solved in isolation from the others, we can, reasonably and logically, expect to see a similar pattern of interconnection among appropriate solutions to our problems. The consciousness of the oneness of mankind is more than just an interconnecting link between various solutions; it is itself the very core of all the solutions. It is, Shoghi Effendi explains, the pivot of the Bahá'í teachings. The importance and significance of this central principle can be illustrated by a simple diagram of a bicycle wheel. The hub of the wheel represents the consciousness of the oneness of humanity. The action that we must take to solve current world problems is rooted in this central principle of oneness just as the spokes of the wheel are firmly anchored into the hub. The analogy is limited in the sense that bicycle spokes are welded into a hub but the principles of justice spring organically out of a central new consciousness of humanity's essential oneness and wholeness. We might also think of the circular rim of the wheel as representing the organically united world which is coming into being as a result of the application of these principles.

These new, universally applicable principles may be identified separately but they must be applied simultaneously to be effective and they must be applied at all levels of life, in our individual actions and at national and international levels. If one spoke of a bicycle wheel is missing or weak, the functioning of the whole wheel is affected. If one of these principles is neglected or omitted, a vital ingredient in the total remedy prepared for the healing of a sick world will be missing. When combined and applied simultaneously the principles complement and reinforce each other and the cumulative effect is powerful and effective.

'. . . thou wilt see', 'Abdu'l-Bahá states, 'that they [these principles] provide an instant remedy for the ailing body of the world.'[3] 'When an illness is slight', He explains, 'a small remedy will suffice to heal it, but when the slight illness becomes a terrible disease, then a very strong remedy must be used by the Divine Healer.'[4]

As change and transformation start at the level of individual thought and consciousness, we shall begin with:

Independent investigation

The powers of investigation into reality, with which each of us is endowed, have, at the beginning of maturity, developed to the point where each person can and must seek out the truth independently and intelligently. The blind acceptance and imitation of ancestral beliefs stunts these emerging powers of our minds and is no longer appropriate to our needs. We must look into all things with a seeing eye, we must see through our own eyes and not through the eyes of others.

> The breeding-ground of all these tragedies is prejudice . . . and the root cause of prejudice is blind imitation of the past . . .[5]

> . . . once every soul inquireth into truth, society will be freed from the darkness of continually repeating the past.[6]

Religion must be the cause of love and unity

'By religion', 'Abdu'l-Bahá explains, 'is meant that which is ascertained by investigation and not that which is based on mere imitation . . .'[7]

During our long infancy, childhood and adolescence we could not see what Bahá'u'lláh has made clear, that the founders of the world's religions are like teachers in the school of the religion of God and that:

> religious truth is not absolute but relative, that Divine Revelation is progessive, not final . . . [that] all established religions [are] divine in origin, identical in their aims, complementary in their functions, continuous in their purpose, indispensable in their value to mankind.[8]

If the nations of the world forsake imitations and investigate the reality underlying the revealed Word of God they will agree and become reconciled.[9]

The harmony of religion and science

Material progress and development alone cannot solve the

problems the world now faces. In fact, such progress is worsening the present situation of injustice, exploitation and environmental degradation. Because of the decay and decline of spiritual values and the consequent rise of material values, technology has become an end in itself and now poses a threat to the very existence of humanity. 'Progress and barbarism', 'Abdu'l-Bahá states, 'go hand in hand, unless material civilization be confirmed by Divine Guidance.'[10]

Religion and science are complementary aspects of one central truth. They are:

the two wings upon which man's intelligence can soar into the heights, with which the human soul can progress. It is not possible to fly with one wing alone! Should a man try to fly with the wing of religion alone he would quickly fall into the quagmire of superstition, whilst on the other hand, with the wing of science alone he would also make no progress, but fall into the despairing slough of materialism.[11]

When religion, shorn of its superstitions, traditions and unintelligent dogmas, shows its conformity with science, then will there be a great unifying, cleansing force ·in the world, which will sweep before it all wars, disagreements, discords and struggles . . .[12]

Elimination of prejudice

Our knowledge and spiritual awareness of the oneness of humanity equip us to eliminate prejudices of all kinds, and the vital impulse of the new revelation creates both the desire and the determination to work at this task and thus move forward to a new level of human unity.

'All prejudices', 'Abdu'l-Bahá states, 'whether of religion, race, politics or nation, must be renounced, for these prejudices have caused the world's sickness.'[13] '. . . if we harbour prejudice it will be the cause of deprivation and ignorance.'[14]

Equality of men and women

'Abdu'l-Bahá states,

> Women have equal rights with men upon earth, in religion
> and in society they are a very important element. As long as
> women are prevented from attaining their highest possi-
> bilities, so long will men be unable to achieve the greatness
> which might be theirs.[15]

The traditional, inherited restrictions which limit development of the capacity of half the human race are now not
merely hindering human progress but helping to imperil all
life on the planet. The over-emphasis on and excessive
development of masculine characteristics have led to wasteful
competition and exploitative technology. The feminine qualities of compassion, tenderness of heart and of reverence for all
forms of existence are urgently needed in all aspects of life.
Women must be given equal rights and opportunities so that
they may make their distinctive and vital contribution to the
healing of the world's sickness. Urgent, emergency measures
must be adopted in families where resources and access to
education are limited. Where there is not enough money to
educate all the children, priority must be given to the
education of girls rather than, as tradition has dictated, to
their brothers.

Universal education

While lip-service is now paid to this principle in many
countries, it is still very far from being achieved and the
number of people in the world who are unable to read or write
is presently increasing. While almost all the world's boys are
getting some form of primary education, enrolment rates for
girls are very low at all levels and two-thirds of the world's
illiterates are women. In Europe and America large sums of

hile almost all the world's boys are getting some form of primary education, enrolment rates for girls are very low

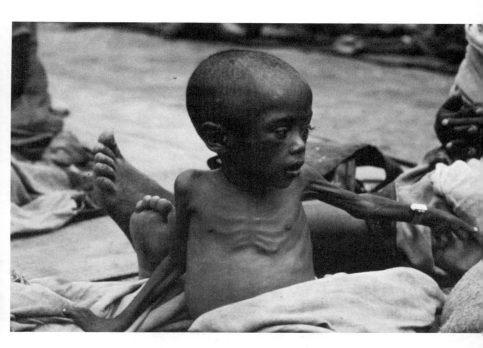

At present more than eight hundred million people are severely undernourished and many millions are actually starving

money are spent on education but increasing numbers of young people leave school without basic literacy skills. The formal educational methods and systems developed in the western world must be examined in the light of the new spiritual principles brought by Bahá'u'lláh and amended where necessary so that all may develop their inner spiritual potential and develop knowledge and skills that will contribute to the happiness of the nations. Material education alone, if divorced from spiritual and ethical foundations is, 'Abdu'l-Bahá warns, of no benefit at all but is, on the contrary, a positive source of harm to humanity.

Elimination of the extremes of wealth and poverty

An obvious consequence of the central principle of oneness is the realization that all people are entitled to live, to have adequate food, clothing and shelter, to receive education and to have meaningful work that will be of benefit to all. 'Nobody should die of hunger . . . one man should not live in excess while another has no possible means of existence.'[16].

At present more than eight hundred million human beings are severely undernourished and many millions are actually starving. The world produces more food per head of population today than ever before in human history but the number of hungry people is increasing rapidly. Less than twenty percent of the world's people now consume more than eighty percent of the planet's resources while the remaining eighty percent are left with less than a twenty percent share. In addition, in an increasing number of countries which are concentrating on material growth, the gap between rich and poor is widening alarmingly. Urgent measures must be taken to eliminate these extremes of superfluity and deprivation both at national and international levels. The vast majority of the world's peoples are prevented from developing their capacities and talents by the inequitable and unjust control and use of the earth's resources. The world body is thus crippled and cannot make healthy progress.

International auxiliary language

The nations of the world must consult together and choose a language which will serve as an international auxiliary language which will be taught as a second language in all schools in all countries. Thus, each child will learn its mother tongue and a second language which will make possible direct communication between peoples. Such a step will provide protection to many minority languages and cultures which are presently threatened with extinction.

Equality before the law

The acceptance of the principle of the oneness of mankind must lead to the legal affirmation of the equality of all people before the law, both at national and international levels. A code of international law listing the essential, universal human rights and obligations must be formulated, observed and, where necessary, enforced.

Collective security

It is now urgently necessary for all countries to join together in establishing an effective system of international security.

'They must', 'Abdu'l-Bahá writes,

> make the Cause of Peace the object of general consultation, and seek by every means in their power to establish a Union of the nations of the world. They must conclude a binding treaty and establish a covenant, the provisions of which shall be sound, inviolable and definite. They must proclaim

it to all the world and obtain for it the sanction of all the human race.[17]

The current dangers of the arms race and the environmental damage now being caused across national boundaries both, in the words of Shoghi Effendi:

... point to the inevitable curtailment of unfettered national sovereignty as an indispensable preliminary to the formation of the future Commonwealth of all the nations of the world.[18]

In the next chapter we shall explore in more detail the urgent need for a genuine international framework which will replace the present structure of competitive power politics through which we attempt, with diminishing success, to run the affairs of our increasingly interdependent world.

18

Collective Security

THE concept of a world federal system, under which all the nations of the world will voluntarily agree to hand over certain of their sovereign rights, still meets with widespread scepticism and scorn. The deeply-held belief in the essential selfishness of individuals is carried to its natural consequence – an acceptance that the present power structures through which the world tries to organize its affairs are fixed and unalterable. Bahá'ís, however, consider that the time for a world federal system is already long overdue and that the acute crises the world is still facing have, in large part, come about precisely because such a system was not brought into being decades ago. In 1931 Shoghi Effendi wrote:

> the fundamental cause of this world unrest is attributable . . . to the failure of those into whose hands the immediate destinies of peoples and nations have been committed, to adjust their system of economic and political institutions to the imperative needs of a rapidly evolving age.[1]

The interdependence of peoples and nations

The central reality of the age in which we live is the interdependence of all peoples and nations. Already, by the early 1930s, the world had become '... contracted and transformed into a single highly complex organism by the marvellous progress achieved in the realm of physical science, by the world-wide expansion of commerce and industry . . .'[2]

Already, by that early date in the present century, there were no longer any isolated national interests. The invention of nuclear weapons has since intensified the need for the nations to create international machinery appropriate to a world in which: 'no national security can be achieved without international security, and no national progress and stability can be achieved without international progress and stability.'[3]

The consequences of the arms race

Increasingly, peoples and governments are realizing that even a limited nuclear exchange could result in a suicidal holocaust for the entire human race. However, the fragile balance of terror still maintained by the nuclear powers, despite recent reductions in arms, does not provide a basis for lasting peace and security but is rather a cause of constant and terrible danger. The continual advances in weapons research and efficiency inexorably increase the dangers of unintentional or accidental nuclear conflict. The idea of nuclear deterrence, on which this precarious balance of terror has until recently been based, is itself fatally flawed. In reality, nuclear and all other armaments are intended as tools that will promote and protect what are thought of as national interests. They must therefore be ready for immediate use in order to be credible deterrents and when they are ready for use they provide no security for any nation but hold the entire world hostage to the imminent threat of nuclear extinction.

Quite apart from the immediate threat to all life that the arms race produces, the increasing contamination of the land, oceans and air and the psychological damage done to all of us who must live with this threatening cloud of extinction hovering over our lives, the steady diversion of more than half the world's resources into military research and hardware, compounds and increases all the other crises the world is now facing. The money which is still poured into weaponry of all kinds produces nothing of direct benefit to humanity but increases scarcity and fuels worldwide inflation. It limits the possibilities of developing peaceful technologies which could bring an end to poverty and disease everywhere. It also limits the possibilities of providing useful and meaningful jobs for unemployed people and is a major cause of high taxation in all countries where such weapons are produced and purchased. As 'Abdu'l-Bahá explained early this century:

> ... every class of society is heavily taxed to feed this insatiable monster of war ... The moral effect of the expenditures of these colossal sums of money for military purposes is just as deteriorating as the actual war and its train of dreadful carnage and horrors.[4]

Obstacles to change

The primary reason why an effective system of collective security has not been put in place is that we are still deeply attached, as individuals and as societies, both emotionally and mentally, to the outdated idea that individual nations can exist and function as absolutely independent sovereign states.

Nation states are not exempt from the process of growth and development which affects all human institutions. In the natural world, even as a flower opens its blossoms to the sun, the seed or fruit which is its purpose and reason for existence is already forming. While the process of nation-building has gone on over many centuries, a slow but steady movement towards a greater unity, a world commonwealth of nations, was already in preparation but is only becoming evident as the process of nation-building itself draws to a close. It is, strikingly, the youngest of the world's nation-states, those which are still suffering from economic oppression and exploitation, that can now see most clearly the need for international structures that will ensure and protect the rights of all nations and peoples. In order to understand more clearly why it is necessary for us to move forward in our thinking we shall take a closer look at the limitations of national sovereignty.

The limitations of national sovereignty

Any social institution, whether it is a family, a town council or a nation-state, exists to serve the interests of the individuals who make up that community. As Aristotle explained over two thousand years ago, the purpose of politics is two-fold: to assure the survival of the members of a society and to give them the opportunity to fulfil themselves as social beings. When the institutions which human beings have devised no longer serve these basic purposes they must be re-evaluated and altered to suit new conditions and circumstances. In the present century, 'Abdu'l-Bahá explains:

> Present exigencies demand new methods of solution; world problems are without precedent . . . Ancient laws and archaic ethical systems will not meet the requirements of modern conditions, for this is clearly the century of a new life.[5]

Nations have, for centuries, used warfare as a means of reaching decisions when they could not agree amongst themselves but in this age of change and renewal, the nature of human warfare has itself undergone a profound change. As a result of advances in the field of science and technology, by the beginning of this century, organized warfare was already an outdated, ineffective and tragically wasteful method of attempting to solve national disagreements and rivalries. Before 1914 'Abdu'l-Bahá explained:

> So perfected has the science of killing become and so efficient the means and instruments of its accomplishment that a whole nation can be obliterated in a short time. Therefore, comparison with the methods and results of ancient warfare is out of the question.[6]

As Jonathan Schell has shown in his book *The Fate of the Earth*, the development of nuclear warfare has made the concept of an entirely independent nation-state completely obsolete. With the advent of nuclear weapons and nuclear power stations, no nation can ensure that it is secure from nuclear devastation, either through war or as a result of an accident. But it is not only nuclear power which limits the concept and the reality of absolute sovereign states. It is the enormous increase in all our technological capacity. We have, like immature adolescents, been using our new-found strength without any accompanying sense of responsibility for our actions. In the last forty years, ecologists now report, we have wrought more damage to the natural systems of the planet than in the preceding stretch of over two million years. The issue we now have to face is:

> not just the desirability but even the feasibility of maintaining an international system that cannot prevent one or several states from damaging the ecological basis for development and even the prospects for survival of any other or even all other states.[7]

Rights and obligations

Freedom is not the last word. Freedom is only part of the story and half of the truth. Freedom is but the negative aspect of the whole phenomenon whose positive aspect is responsibleness.[8]

This unrestrained use of enormous power illustrates the deeper obstacle to change which is impeding progress in the field of disarmament. It is, in itself, a symptom of our growth through adolescence to our collective maturity. With all the vehemence and enthusiasm of youth we have identified and demanded our inalienable rights – the right to freedom and speech and belief and the right to freedom from fear and want – but we are still in the process of realizing that our rights are only one side of the coin of our maturity. We will not begin to achieve them until we understand that they carry with them certain vital obligations.

When we were children we sometimes idly imagined that once we were grown up we would be able to do exactly as we liked. But even as children we had to learn that there are only certain places where it is safe to cross a street and that it is necessary, daily, to take into account the needs and rights of other members of our family. Our international obligations are new and unfamiliar but they are being brought home to us by our present perils and by the painful realization that only by cooperating at an international level can we achieve any safety or security. As Edwin Reischauer, a Harvard professor and former diplomat, explains, we have to make a considerable mental adjustment and appreciate that, in the new circumstances of an interdependent world, 'The basic unit of human cooperation and hence survival is moving from the national to the global level.'[9]

The competition of our adolescence and the power structures that it threw up have outlived their usefulness and their perpetuation is now causing immense damage to our planetary home, limiting all our possibilities for future healthy growth and, consequently, hindering progress towards the achievement of all our rights. The existing economic system of the world, whereby the industrialized nations exploit for their own benefit the resources of the developing world, is rapidly increasing inequality and producing famine and deprivation. The present injustices which have arisen from this competition and exploitation will inevitably lead to war unless corrective measures are now taken. Furthermore, ecologists warn, if we continue to exploit and disrupt the planet's natural systems as we are presently doing, we will bring extinction on ourselves without ever firing a single nuclear weapon.

The obligation and responsibility of our emerging maturity is to create an international system which enables nations to settle disputes without the use of force, which will close the widening gap between the 'rich' and 'poor' nations and promote environmental protection and sustainable development. But it is not realistic to expect nations to give up their rights to make war and to promote what they perceive as their 'national interests' unless an alternative framework for action is available to them.

Fear of a world tyranny

Many people are opposed to any scheme for world federalism because they fear that it could rapidly turn into world tyranny. However, the history of the 1920s and 1930s demonstrates that the opportunity for several nations to attempt world domination arose precisely because the political will to devise effective safeguards against aggression and to make them work was entirely lacking in all nations. After 1945, although the United Nations Organization was brought into existence, the nations were still not willing to abandon the concept of absolute national sovereignty. They were, therefore, obliged to waste the time, energy and resources of their people in senseless, profitless and extremely hazardous competition. The present lack of effective inter-national safeguards against aggression continues to provide excellent opportunities for the establishment of a world tyranny. As Edwin Reischauer observed in 1974:

> . . . traditional balance of power concepts do not have much relevance today. Our attention and efforts in international relations have been seriously misdirected. The present world situation has evolved far away from that of the eighteenth and nineteenth centuries, when the great bulk of the relations between nations had to do with the possibili-ties and realities of war.[10]

Once again, we are drawn back to the inseparability of war and the concept of the absolute nation-state and are obliged to recognize the inadequacy of the present structures to meet our needs. Over a century ago, Bahá'u'lláh wrote:

> The signs of impending convulsions and chaos can now be discerned, inasmuch as the prevailing order appeareth to be lamentably defective.[11]

A communication gap

The outdated idea that human beings are innately aggressive is still a major obstacle to change and it fuels the vicious circle of pessimism that runs between leaders and their peoples. Many leaders dare not promote openly the abandonment of a narrow nationalism for fear of losing the support of their people. Ordinary citizens, on the other hand, growing increasingly concerned by the deteriorating condition of the planet, perceive their politicians as selfish and short-sighted.

However, as the hearts and minds of people everywhere are freed from the emotional and intellectual constraint imposed by a belief in humanity's innate selfishness and aggressiveness, the realization will dawn that it is now not only possible but absolutely necessary, in the interest of human survival, to create new institutions at all levels that are 'at once progressive and peaceful, dynamic and harmonious . . . giving free play to individual creativity and initiative but based on co-operation and reciprocity.'[12]

An organic process

In 1875 'Abdu'l-Bahá wrote:

> The world of politics is like the world of man; he is seed at first, and then passes by degrees to the condition of embryo and foetus, acquiring a bone structure, being clothed with flesh, taking on his own special form . . . Just as this is a requirement of creation and is based on the universal Wisdom, the political world in the same way cannot instantaneously evolve from the nadir of defectiveness to the zenith of rightness and perfection.[13]

This immense process, whereby we have to raise our focus from a national to an international level in order to solve problems at every level, mirrors the earlier movements towards national unity which made possible the establishment of nation-states. As Shoghi Effendi suggests:

> [In the movements towards unity] are we not witnessing the repetition, on a larger scale, of those stirring struggles and fierce controversies that preceded the birth, and assisted in the reconstruction, of the unified nations of the West?[14]

He also observes that just as the first stirrings of nationalism were stamped on in earlier times, so too, the

> champions of an unfettered national sovereignty, in their turn, have laboured and are still labouring to discredit principles upon which their own salvation must ultimately depend.[15]

The steady, organic growth towards a larger unity and a wider loyalty than has yet animated the human race is not, as Edwin Reischauer observes,

> a simple, one-step achievement, any more than the development of the nation-state was . . . the creation of a world community will be a multi-faceted and complex process, spanning a wide variety of human activities and requiring a great number of inter-related steps.[16]

The watchword of Bahá'u'lláh's design for world unity is 'unity in diversity' and its purpose is:

> neither to stifle the flame of a sane and intelligent patriotism in men's hearts, nor to abolish the system of national autonomy so essential if the evils of excessive centralization are to be avoided.[17]

Understanding that the growth process is an organic one, Bahá'ís know that the diversity of the human race is a source of strength but that the imperative overall need for the security which will allow our survival demands that national impulses and interests be subordinated 'to the imperative claims of a unified world'.[18]

While the process of growth is a gradual one, there are in nature periods of sudden organic development: the opening of a bud, the cracking open of a fruit or seed-pod. In the same way the world of humanity is now at such a crisis point when decisive choices have to be made. Can we risk the continuance of the present system of struggle, competition and conflict, or can we move forward to a new era when we build institutions appropriate to our common need for survival?

'There is no more urgent task in the quest for peace', the Club of Rome reported over a decade ago, 'than to help guide the world system onto the path of organic growth through the various stages of its evolution through cooperation rather than confrontation.'[18]

The principle of collective security

> In the light of new knowledge, a world authority and an
> eventual world state are not just *desirable* in the name of
> brotherhood, they are *necessary* for survival.[20]

In 1875, 'Abdu'l-Bahá wrote a detailed account of a system of
international collective security. He said that the leaders and
rulers of the nations must:

> seek by every means in their power to establish a Union of
> the nations of the world. They must conclude a binding
> treaty and establish a covenant, the provisions of which
> shall be sound, inviolable and definite. They must proclaim
> it to all the world and obtain for it the sanction of all the
> human race ... All the forces of humanity must be
> mobilized to ensure the stability and permanence of this
> Most Great Covenant. In this all-embracing Pact the limits
> and frontiers of each and every nation should be clearly
> fixed, the principles underlying the relations of govern-
> ments towards one another definitely laid down, and all
> international agreements and obligations ascertained. In
> like manner, the size of the armaments of every government
> should be strictly limited, for if the preparations for war and
> the military forces of any nation should be allowed to
> increase, they will arouse the suspicion of others. The
> fundamental principle underlying this solemn Pact should
> be so fixed that if any government later violate any one of its
> provisions, all the governments on earth should arise to
> reduce it to utter submission, nay the human race as a
> whole should resolve, with every power at its disposal, to
> destroy that government. Should this greatest of all
> remedies be applied to the sick body of the world, it will
> assuredly recover from its ills and will remain eternally safe
> and secure.[21]

Disarmament and human rights

Obviously, this basis of peace will not be a sound one unless the leaders and rulers are themselves governing their own countries justly, unless they are allowing their own citizens to enjoy the basic human rights: freedom from fear and want and freedom of conscience and belief. The movement towards peace and justice in the international context can only progress to the degree that these rights are permitted in all countries. We can therefore see a two-fold process of transformation going on, purging and reshaping humanity at national and international levels, as the community of nations struggles towards both stability and justice.

In 1912 'Abdu'l-Bahá explained that:

Among the results of the manifestation of spiritual forces will be that the human world will adapt itself to a new social form, the justice of God will become manifest throughout human affairs, and human equality will be universally established.[22]

Elements of world order

It is as a global species that we are transforming the planet. It is only as a global species – pooling our knowledge coordinating our actions and sharing what the planet has to offer – that we have any prospect for managing the planet's transformation along pathways of sustainable development. Self-conscious, intelligent management of the earth is one of the great challenges facing humanity as it approaches the twenty-first century.[23]

Since the interdependence of all peoples and nations is the central reality of our age, we need to bring into being institutions which reflect that reality. The establishment of the

League of Nations and later the United Nations were both essential, preliminary steps in the process of constructing a world federal system.

The current crises afflicting the world's climate, the threatened collapse of its economic system, the threats of terrorism, of drug addiction and the spread of AIDS are, in addition to the nuclear peril, forcing the nations to act as one. The world is, as Shoghi Effendi wrote, being propelled towards unity by forces over which it has no control. To meet the challenges of all the present crises, the nations are discovering that they cannot act effectively until they agree to create,

Some form of a world Super-State . . . in whose favour all the nations of the world will have willingly ceded every claim to make war, certain rights to impose taxation and all rights to maintain armaments, except for purposes of maintaining internal order within their respective dominions. Such a state will have to include within its orbit

- an International Executive adequate to enforce supreme and unchallengeable authority on every recalcitrant member of the commonwealth;
- a World Parliament whose members shall be elected by the people in their respective countries and whose election shall be confirmed by their respective governments;
- and a Supreme Tribunal whose judgement will have a binding effect even in such cases where the parties concerned did not voluntarily agree to submit their case to its consideration.
- A world community in which all economic barriers will have been permanently demolished and the interdependence of Capital and Labour definitely recognized;
- in which the clamour of religious fanaticism and strife will have been forever stilled;

- in which the flame of racial animosity will have been finally extinguished;
- in which a single code of international law – the product of the considered judgement of the world's federated representatives – shall have as its sanction the instant and coercive intervention of the combined forces of the federated units;
- and finally a world community in which the fury of a capricious and militant nationalism will have been transmuted into an abiding consciousness of world citizenship

such indeed, appears, in its broadest outline, the Order anticipated by Bahá'u'lláh, an Order that shall come to be regarded as the fairest fruit of a slowly maturing age.[24]

But how, we must now ask, how on earth are we going to do all this? Even if we can now understand how necessary it is to create a genuine international framework for action, are we really capable of doing such a thing? How can we bring about these vast, planetary adjustments when we can't even manage our own family, neighbourhood and local affairs in harmony?

To answer this most sensible question, we must explore another facet of Bahá'u'lláh's teachings – the Bahá'í principles and methods of consultation. Bahá'í consultation is, as we shall discover, a new and unique form of collective investigation and problem-solving which is ideally suited to the urgent needs of our time.

19

Consultation

A Tool for Maturity

'ALL created things', 'Abdu'l-Bahá writes, 'have their degree or stage of maturity. The period of maturity in the life of a tree is the time of its fruit-bearing . . . and in the human kingdom man reaches his maturity when the light of his intelligence attains its greatest power and development.'[1]

Our knowledge of the oneness of humanity, of the interdependence and interconnection of all life forms and our growing awareness of the oneness of religion all attest to our emerging collective maturity. These gifts of maturity are already creating in us new abilities and capacities for collective decision-making and problem-solving at every level of human affairs. They will soon enable us to cooperate in areas of life where we have long imagined cooperation and collaboration to be utterly impossible.

'Consultation', Bahá'u'lláh states, 'is a shining light which, in a dark world, leadeth the way and guideth. For everything there is and will continue to be a station of perfection and maturity. The maturity of the gift of understanding is made manifest through consultation.'[2]

The word 'consultation' has been in our vocabulary for a long time and we can read in a dictionary that it means 'to consult together, to consider, to deliberate'. We have been trying to do this, to the best of our developing ability, throughout human history. Now, on the threshold of our collective maturity and equipped with the guidance contained in Bahá'u'lláh's teachings, we can begin to discover the depths of the true meaning of this familiar word and catch a glimpse of the tremendous possibilities of mature consultation.

Bahá'í consultation is at once both a process of spiritual growth and a practical tool of decision-making. It demands a spiritual effort from each person present. It requires that all struggle for humility, that all realize the limitations of their individual viewpoints and thoughts, and that all consciously strive to open their minds to the thoughts of others. It necessitates that we purify our own motives and detach ourselves from all ideas of our own importance and essential rightness. It is rooted in the knowledge and understanding that there is an inexhaustible source of goodness and wisdom which we can draw on increasingly as we learn to work together. It is also built on the conviction that the ultimate good of all the individual members of a community and of the whole world-body of peoples and nations will only be achieved through the achievement of the good of the whole. It rests on the assurance that as we strive for the necessary detachment, we will gradually acquire the patience, self-discipline and sensitivity to others that is required. There are, however, certain basic requirements which must be met before mature and fruitful consultation can occur. These requirements stem from the following principles.

Groups, not individuals; service, not power

A major limitation of childhood and youth is that we were not, during those stages of life, in possession of enough facts and knowledge to make mature decisions. In the complex, interwoven world of the late twentieth century, no one individual can hope to have access to all the information needed. This is why Bahá'ís are instructed by Bahá'u'lláh to work together in groups for it is now only a group of people, working to cover all aspects of each issue, that can provide a wide enough perspective of any issue of concern to a community.

As we move out of an era of prolonged competition into one of mutual and worldwide cooperation, a new concept of leadership is emerging. We have already seen that a belief in the inevitability of war is a limited, adolescent interpretation of world affairs. Similarly, we can now, by applying the principles of mature consultation, move away from the limitations of power-oriented, competitive and divisive methods of decision-making and thus leave behind us the conflicts of both factions and individuals that have so hindered collective investigation and problem-solving up to this time. But to do this each one of us must strive for a greater measure of individual maturity.

The important point to remember is that the keynote of the age which has already been born is service to the whole of humanity. Any action which is based on promoting the welfare of only one section of humanity at the expense of others will only produce further problems. In addition, as a result of the incredible progress achieved in the fields of science and technology, we have at our disposal the power either to make the earth unfit for human and animal habitation or to enhance our own habitat for the benefit of future generations. We have to consider from the very start of any consultation what impact any projected action will have on our environment so that our power will be used to protect and enhance our resources instead of destroying them.

Universal participation

In Bahá'í administration, decisions are made by groups of people who have been democratically elected by the whole community. However, a fundamental prerequisite of effective consultation and decision-making is that all those who are affected by a decision must have an opportunity to participate, freely and frankly, in the consultative process. All must be enabled to contribute their views and wishes to a decision-making group. Much of the frustration and apathy which exists in organized societies, whether of the east or the west, arises because ordinary people do not have sufficient opportunity to express their own views and because even when they do have such an opportunity their views are all too often ignored and rejected in favour of the vested interests of the rich or powerful.

Detachment

In childhood and early youth we often accepted the opinions or attitudes of other people simply because of our strong emotional attachments to the people holding these views. But as we grow towards maturity we realize that we can no longer do this, we must now see and think for ourselves. When we meet to consult with others we must learn to consider all the ideas and suggestions put forward on their own merits and without attachment to or prejudice against the person who is expressing them. The idea itself is what matters, not the personality or circumstances of the person expressing it.

If we wish to give a just and fair hearing to the ideas being expressed, we must learn to totally disregard every circumstance connected with the individuals contributing them, whether they are rich or poor, whether they have gone through a lengthy academic training or are illiterate, whether we have often disagreed with them in the past, whether they are men or women, young or old, etc. If we give our attention to these matters, our view of the essential idea being expressed becomes distorted and we are unable to give it a fair hearing.

Similarly, when we ourselves contribute ideas, views or opinions to a discussion, we must learn to detach ourselves from the ideas we put forward. We must learn to give them freely, to put them on the table with all the others for in so doing we can acquire the freedom to consider our own ideas objectively. Once we have given our idea to the whole group it is no longer ours at all. Therefore we do not have to defend or justify it against everyone else's ideas. We are not engaged in winning anything or in beating others; we are there to find the best possible solution and everyone has something to contribute to it, provided that each person learns to let go of his or her particular contribution and allow it to be worked on with all the others.

Courtesy and moderation

In such consultation everyone must be courteous and considerate of other people's views and all must put forward their ideas with moderation without belittling the thoughts of others or hurting the feelings of anyone present. Sarcasm, scorn, contempt and one-upmanship have no place in mature consultation for they lead immediately to alienation and resentment and produce only damage in human affairs. This emphasis on courtesy and consideration gives rise to an atmosphere in which everyone can express themselves fully and frankly without the fear of jeopardizing existing friendships or creating personal antagonisms.

These basic, preliminary principles help to prepare us for genuine consultation as each one helps to build a situation in which there can be a constructive clash of ideas and opinions without an accompanying clash of personalities but rather with a steady increase of trust, confidence and harmony amongst those consulting together. Ideas are bound to clash and 'Abdu'l-Bahá tells us that they must do so for 'the shining spark of truth cometh forth only after the clash of differing opinions.'[3]

It is from this frank and unfettered mingling of many elements that, as Bahá'ís have discovered, new insights, new concepts and new solutions emerge which are not stale compromises but are new, imaginative solutions to difficult problems. When those consulting together genuinely strive to acquire the necessary spiritual qualities, new creative energies which potentially exist within every human being, are released in human consciousness.

The willing acceptance of majority decisions

When Bahá'ís work together in spiritual assemblies and need to decide on specific courses of action, another important principle comes into play. As they develop their consultative skills, they often find that they can make unanimous decisions, although sometimes they need to vote on issues. 'Abdu'l-Bahá stresses that every person participating in the consultation must willingly and joyfully accept the decision of the majority, even if he or she spoke against it during the consultation. Once such a majority decision is reached, no one must criticize it but all must work to carry it out. All the individuals in the community who are affected by the decision must also work to put it into practice willingly and joyfully.

There is, 'Abdu'l-Bahá explains, a very important reason for this. If everyone works together to carry out a decision, then, if it is indeed mistaken, the error will soon be discovered. The matter can quickly be brought back to the attention of the assembly and the mistake can be corrected. But if some people act to carry out the decision and others do not, then it will not be clear what went wrong – was it the decision itself or was it because some people did not take the action that was being asked of them? 'Abdu'l-Bahá gives a clear warning that 'stubbornness and persistence in one's views will lead ultimately to discord and wrangling and the truth will remain hidden.'[4]

Careful evaluation and monitoring

Once decisions have been made and put into practice, they must be constantly monitored and re-evaluated in the light of their consequences. This is often very difficult to do under confrontational systems of decision-making where individuals have been forced to uphold and defend their views against all others. But in Bahá'í administration, where there is this essential separation between ideas and the people expressing them, it is much easier to evaluate decisions and, where necessary, alter them in the light of new knowledge and experience.

Literacy is not essential

Although consultation can improve and be greatly enriched when those consulting are able to read and write, the lack of literacy does not prevent Bahá'ís from learning to consult together, for consultation is not an elitist skill which requires formal, western education and the acquisition of diplomas. Indeed, many cultures outside the dominant western culture have practised various forms of community consultation and consensus decision-making for a long time. When they have access to the Bahá'í teachings they are able to build on what already exists in their own cultures instead of seeing them swamped and extinguished by alien, divisive methods of decision-making that split and polarize their communities. In the experience of Bahá'ís, it is usually the societies outside the dominant materialist culture which can most rapidly benefit from the new principles of consultation because they are not handicapped by the egocentrism of western culture.

The contribution of women

In many traditional societies decision-making has been, and often still is, the province of men alone. It is now widely recognized by many governments that it is absolutely necessary to involve both women and men in all levels of consultation and decision-making. As Bahá'ís strive to put into practice Bahá'u'lláh's teachings, and as they apply them to their decision-making, they are able to overcome long-established customs and traditions that have denied women any role in decision-making.

The keystone

All these principles which have been listed are, one by one, already being recognized by many groups and individuals as essential elements of successful problem-solving in today's world. There is yet one remaining which, in the experience of Bahá'ís, is the keystone of the whole structure. In all their consultation, from an individual to an international level, Bahá'ís refer to the writings of Bahá'u'lláh and 'Abdu'l-Bahá in order to identify all the spiritual principles which are relevant to issues under discussion and to draw on the wealth of spiritual guidance which these writings provide. As 'Abdu'l-Bahá explains:

> Naught but the celestial potency of the Word of God, which ruleth and transcendeth the realities of all things, is capable

of harmonizing the divergent thoughts, sentiments, ideas
and convictions of the children of men.[5]

This constant refreshment and renewal which comes from
exposure to the spiritual teachings which have been given to
help humanity through the difficult transition from youth to
maturity enables Bahá'ís to reorient their lives and their
actions around a spiritual axis rather than a material one, to
move away from the competitive struggle for existence and the
exploitation both of planetary resources and of peoples that
this struggle has brought on us and rapidly to advance the
work of building a new world order based on mutual
cooperation and reciprocity in which there is a just and
equitable sharing of the earth's resources.

As Bahá'ís practise these new arts and skills of consultation,
they are becoming increasingly aware of the benefits such arts
and skills bring to all. Bahá'ís are confident that they will be of
immeasurable assistance in the wide-ranging international
consultations which must take place as the nations begin the
vital task of global demilitarization and reconstruction. The
Universal House of Justice, in its letter of 1985 addressed to
all the peoples of the world states:

> The very attempt to achieve peace through the consultative
> action he [Bahá'u'lláh] proposed can release such a
> salutary spirit among the peoples of the earth that no power
> could resist the final, triumphal outcome.[6]

Bahá'ís are encouraged to work in groups

'The gift of God to this enlightened age is the knowledge of the oneness of mankind

20

The Way Ahead

As we draw near to the end of this brief exploration of peace-building from a Bahá'í perspective, we can see that the journey is, in itself, a prologue to a much vaster and far-stretching journey, the momentous journeying of all the world's peoples towards peace. Simply by being alive today we are privileged to join in the journey at what is, perhaps, its most dramatic and thrilling moment, the moment when we begin to see that peace is, finally, attainable, the moment when

> The Great Peace towards which people of good will throughout the centuries have inclined their hearts, of which seers and poets for countless generations have expressed their vision, and for which from age to age the sacred scriptures of mankind have constantly held the promise, is now at long last within the reach of the nations.[1]

The spirit released into the world by Bahá'u'lláh is now purging and reshaping the whole of humanity, restoring vision and hope to individual lives and reshaping human institutions to match the reality of our age – the oneness and wholeness of the entire human race. There are convulsive changes still ahead of us and the crises the nations now face are clear warnings of the urgent need to transform our innermost thoughts and all our actions. In the guidance provided by Bahá'u'lláh, the latest of God's Messengers, we can find the quickest and the safest route out of our present dangers.

There is no time in a book of this length to write of the life of Bahá'u'lláh, of His imprisonment and exile, nor of those who have given their energy and their resources and even life itself that this message may renew the earth. There is no room to explore in any detail the remarkable world community of diverse peoples which has come into being as a result of Bahá'u'lláh's life, nor the unique administrative order which He outlined and which acts as a channel for the flow of His teachings through the world. These journeys of discovery lie ahead.

21

The Hour of Unity

'TODAY the light of Truth is shining upon the world in its abundance; the breezes of the heavenly garden are blowing throughout all regions; the call of the Kingdom is heard in all lands, and the breath of the Holy Spirit is felt in all hearts that are faithful. The Spirit of God is giving eternal life. In this wonderful age the East is enlightened, the West is fragrant, and everywhere the soul inhales the holy perfume. The sea of the unity of mankind is lifting up its waves with joy, for there is real communication between the hearts and minds of men. . .

'This is a new cycle of human power. All the horizons of the world are luminous, and the world will become indeed as a garden and a paradise. It is the hour of unity of the sons of men and of the drawing together of all races and all classes. You are loosed from ancient superstitions which have kept men ignorant, destroying the foundations of true humanity.

'The gift of God to this enlightened age is the knowledge of the oneness of mankind and of the fundamental oneness of religion. War shall cease between nations, and by the will of God the Most Great Peace shall come. . .'[1]

'Abdu'l-Bahá

References

Frontispiece
1. Bahá'u'lláh, *Peace*, p. 7.
2. The Universal House of Justice, *Promise*, p. 3.

1. Introduction
1. The Universal House of Justice, *Promise*, p. 1.
2. Bahá'u'lláh, *Peace*, p. 7.
3. Bahá'u'lláh, cited in Shoghi Effendi, *God Passes By*, p. 217.

2. A Special Time
1. In his annual report to the UN General Assembly.
2. 'Abdu'l-Bahá, *Paris Talks*, p. 29.
3. 'Abdu'l-Bahá, *Promulgation*, p. 145.

3. Problem-Solving
1. 'Abdu'l-Bahá, *Foundations*, p. 101.

4. Human Problems
1. Capra, *Turning Point*, p. 69.
2. Mesarovic and Pestel, *Mankind at the Turning Point*, pp. 1–2.
3. Bahá'u'lláh, *Tablets*, p. 67.

5. Gaining a Perspective
1. Shoghi Effendi, *Promised Day is Come*, pp. 121–2.
2. The Universal House of Justice, *Promise*, p. 3.

6. A Dilemma and a Challenge
1. Macey, *Despair*, p. 19.

7. The Need to Know
1. 'Abdu'l-Bahá, *Selections*, p. 246.
2. Shakespeare, *Hamlet*, Act II, Sc. 2.
3. Shakespeare, *Lear*, Act III, Sc. 5.
4. Bahá'u'lláh, *Gleanings*, p. 97.
5. Leakey, *Making of Mankind*, p. 21.

8. The Reality of Man
1. 'Abdu'l-Bahá, *Promulgation*, p. 227.
2. Bahá'u'lláh, *Gleanings*, p. 49.
3. 'Abdu'l-Bahá, *Promulgation*, p. 297.
4. 'Abdu'l-Bahá, *Selections*, p. 27.
5. ibid. p. 48.
6. ibid. p. 157.
7. Bahá'u'lláh, *Gleanings*, pp. 158–9.
8. 'Abdu'l-Bahá, *Paris Talks*, p. 91.
9. 'Abdu'l-Bahá, *Promulgation*, p. 178.
10. 'Abdu'l-Bahá, *Selections*, p. 263.
11. Ghiglieri, *Chimpanzees*, p. 87.
12. Goodall, *Chimpanzees of Gombe*, p. 592.
13. ibid.
14. 'Abdu'l-Bahá, *Paris Talks*, p. 60.
15. 'Abdu'l-Bahá, *Some Answered Questions*, pp. 235–6.

9. A Unique Predicament
1. Morgan, *Aquatic Ape*, p. 112.
2. Leakey, *Making of Mankind*, p. 11.
3. Bahá'u'lláh, *Tablets*, p. 67.
4. 'Abdu'l-Bahá, *Selections*, pp. 287–8.
5. 'Abdu'l-Bahá, *Promulgation*, p. 109.
6. ibid, p. 302.
7. Bahá'u'lláh, *Gleanings*, p. 77.
8. ibid. p. 194.
9. 'Abdu'l-Bahá, *Selections*, p. 181.
10. 'Abdu'l-Bahá, *Foundations*, p. 48.
11. 'Abdu'l-Bahá, *Promulgation*, p. 262.

12. 'Abdu'l-Bahá, *Some Answered Questions*, p. 78.
13. 'Abdu'l-Bahá, *Promulgation*, p. 262.
14. 'Abdu'l-Bahá, *Foundations*, p. 48.
15. ibid. p. 60.
16. Bahá'u'lláh, *Hidden Words*, Arabic no. 19.
17. 'Abdu'l-Bahá, *Foundations*, pp. 42–3.
18. Jane Goodall, interview with Polly Toynbee, *Manchester Guardian Weekly*, 25 January 1987, p. 19.
19. Frankl, *Unconscious God*, p. 96.
20. Menuhin, *Unfinished Journey*, p. 430.
21. 'Abdu'l-Bahá, *Secret of Divine Civilization*, pp. 23–4.
22. Moody, *Light Beyond*, pp. 33–6.

10. An Error Exposed
1. Chief Sealth (Seattle) of Washington State in an address to a delegation of white men who wished to purchase his people's tribal lands in 1854.
2. *See* Robert Ardrey, *African Genesis* and *Territorial Imperative*.
3. Lancaster, *Primate Behaviour*, p. 1.
4. Thomas, 'Are We Fit to Fit In?', cited in *Beyond War*, p. 7.
5. Montagu, *Man and Aggression*, pp. 1–16.
6. Robertson, *Sociology*, p. 60.
7. ibid.
8. ibid. p. 61.
9. 'Abdu'l-Bahá, *Promulgation*, p. 60.
10. Salk, 'A Conversation', cited in *Beyond War*, p. 7.

11. Discovering Our Past
1. Leakey, *Human Origins*, p. 24.
2. 'Children of Eve', WGBH Educational Foundation, pp. 7–10.
3. Lovejoy, 'Evolution of Human Walking', *Scientific American*, November 1988, pp. 118–25.
4. ibid. p. 125.
5. Leakey, *Human Origins*, p. 61.
6. Hobbs, *Leviathan*.
7. ibid.

8. Isaac, 'Food-Sharing', *Scientific American*, April 1979, p. 102.
9. *New Scientist*, 28 July 1988.
10. Montagu, *Man and Aggression*, p. 16.
11. ibid. p. 6.
12. Isaac, 'Food-Sharing', *Scientific American*, April 1979, p. 102.
13. Tanner, *On Becoming Human*. pp. 222, 268.

12. Cooperation and Food-Sharing
1. Lancaster, *Primate Behaviour*, p. 4.
2. Isaac, 'Food-Sharing', *Scientific American*, April 1979, p. 92.
3. ibid. p. 94.
4. ibid. p. 93.
5. ibid. p. 102.
6. 'Abdu'l-Bahá, *Promulgation*, p. 103.
7. Frayer, Horton, Macchiarellir and Muss, *Nature*, vol. 330, 5 November 1987.
8. U Thant, *Portfolio for Peace*.
9. 'Abdu'l-Bahá, *Foundations*, p. 38.
10. 'Abdu'l-Bahá, *Selections*, p. 289.

13. The Cause of the Present Crisis
1. *Our Common Future*, p. 4.
2. 'Abdu'l-Bahá, *Paris Talks*, p. 17.
3. Russell, *Has Man a Future?*, p. 45.
4. *Beyond War*, p. 1.
5. Shoghi Effendi, cited in *Lights of Guidance*, no. 279, p. 94.
6. 'Abdu'l-Bahá, *Promulgation*, p. 305.

14. The Essential Connection
1. Bahá'u'lláh, cited in Shoghi Effendi, *World Order*, p. 60.
2. 'Abdu'l-Bahá, *Foundations*, p. 58.
3. 'Abdu'l-Bahá, *Promulgation*, p. 296.
4. ibid. p. 295.
5. ibid. p. 463.
6. Bahá'u'lláh, *Gleanings*, p. 50.
7. 'Abdu'l-Bahá, *Selections*, p. 34.
8. Bahá'u'lláh, *Gleanings*, pp. 47–8.

9. ibid. p. 81.
10. 'Abdu'l-Bahá, *Promulgation*, p. 140.
11. 'Abdu'l-Bahá, *Selections*, p. 52.
12. ibid. p. 58.

15. Coming of Age
1. Bahá'u'lláh, cited in Shoghi Effendi, *World Order*, p. 169.
2. Shoghi Effendi, ibid., p. 43.
3. ibid. p. 163.
4. The Universal House of Justice, *Promise*, pp. 3–4.
5. 'Abdu'l-Bahá, cited in Shoghi Effendi, *World Order*, pp. 38–9.
6. *Our Common Future*, p. 27.
7. 'Abdu'l-Bahá, cited in Shoghi Effendi, *World Order*, p. 165.

16. The Key to Peace
1. Einstein, cited in *Beyond War*, p. 8.
2. 'Abdu'l-Bahá, cited in *Bahá'í Revelation*, p. 280.
3. 'Abdu'l-Bahá, *Selections*, p. 31.
4. 'Abdu'l-Bahá, *Promulgation*, pp. 144–5.
5. 'Abdu'l-Bahá, *Selections*, p. 244.
6. Chief Seattle/Sealth, 1858.
7. Schell, *Fate of the Earth*, p. 91.
8. Hoyle, cited in *Beyond War*, p. 29.
9. 'Abdu'l-Bahá, *Foundations*, p. 21.
10. 'Abdu'l-Bahá, *Selections*, p. 297.
11. Bahá'u'lláh, *Tablets*, p. 84.
12. ibid. pp. 87–8.
13. 'Abdu'l-Bahá, *Selections*, p. 1.
14. Shoghi Effendi, *World Order*, pp. 197–8.
15. 'Abdu'l-Bahá, cited in *Bahá'í Revelation*, p. 289.
16. 'Abdu'l-Bahá, *Paris Talks*, pp. 52–3.
17. Bahá'u'lláh, *Gleanings*, p. 215.
18. 'Abdu'l-Bahá, cited in *Bahá'í Revelation*, pp. 287–8.

17. Essential Building-Blocks
1. 'Abdu'l-Bahá, *Foundations*, p. 83.
2. 'Abdu'l-Bahá, *Selections*, p. 253.

3. ibid. p. 59.
4. 'Abdu'l-Bahá, *Paris Talks*, p. 27.
5. 'Abdu'l-Bahá, *Selections*, p. 247.
6. ibid. p. 248.
7. ibid. p. 303.
8. Shoghi Effendi, *World Order*, p. 58.
9. 'Abdu'l-Bahá, *Foundations*, p. 84.
10. 'Abdu'l-Bahá, *Selections*, p. 284.
11. 'Abdu'l-Bahá, *Paris Talks*, p. 143.
12. ibid. p. 146.
13. ibid.
14. 'Abdu'l-Bahá, *Foundations*, p. 15.
15. 'Abdu'l-Bahá, *Bahá'í Revelation*, pp. 291–2.
16. 'Abdu'l-Bahá, *Paris Talks*, p. 132.
17. 'Abdu'l-Bahá, *Secret of Divine Civilization*, p. 64.
18. Shoghi Effendi, *World Order*, p. 40.

18. Collective Security

1. Shoghi Effendi, *World Order*, p. 36.
2. ibid. p. 47.
3. U Thant, *Portfolio for Peace*, p. 78.
4. 'Abdu'l-Bahá, cited in *Star of the West*, vol. V, no. 8, p. 115.
5. 'Abdu'l-Bahá, *Promulgation*, p. 140.
6. ibid. p. 124.
7. *Our Common Future*, p. 313.
8. Frankl, *Man's Search for Meaning*, p. 209.
9. Reischauer, *Towards the 21st Century*.
10. ibid. p. 51.
11. Bahá'u'lláh, *Gleanings*, p. 216.
12. The Universal House of Justice, *Promise*, p. 3.
13. 'Abdu'l-Bahá, *Secret of Divine Civilization*, 107.
14. Shoghi Effendi, *World Order*, pp. 44–5.
15. ibid. p. 44.
16. Reischauer, *Towards the 21st Century*, p. 90.
17. Shoghi Effendi, *World Order*, p. 41.
18. ibid. p. 42.

19. Mesarovic and Pestel, *Man at the Turning Point*, p. 146.
20. Albert Einstein, cited in *Beyond War*, p. 21.
21. 'Abdu'l-Bahá, *Secret of Divine Civilization*, pp. 64–5.
22. 'Abdu'l-Bahá, *Promulgation*, p. 132.
23. Clark, 'Managing Planet Earth', *Scientific American*, September 1989, p. 47.
24. Shoghi Effendi, *World Order*, pp. 40–1 (emphasis added).

19. Consultation
1. 'Abdu'l-Bahá, cited in Shoghi Effendi, *World Order*, p. 164.
2. Bahá'u'lláh, cited in *Heaven*, p. 3.
3. 'Abdu'l-Bahá, cited in ibid. p. 5.
4. ibid. p. 6.
5. 'Abdu'l-Bahá, cited in Shoghi Effendi, *World Order*, p. 42.
6. The Universal House of Justice, *Promise*, p. 20.

20. The Way Ahead
1. The Universal House of Justice, *Promise*, p. 1.

21. The Hour of Unity
1. 'Abdu'l-Bahá, cited in *Bahá'í Revelation*, p. 280.

Bibliography

'Abdu'l-Bahá. *Foundations of World Unity*. Wilmette, Illinois: Bahá'í Publishing Trust, 1974.

——*Paris Talks*. Oakham: Bahá'í Publishing Trust, 1969.

——*The Promulgation of Universal Peace*. Compiled by Howard MacNutt. Wilmette, Illinois: Bahá'í Publishing Trust, 2nd ed. 1982.

——*The Secret of Divine Civilization*. Translated from the original Persian text by Marzieh Gail. Wilmette, Illinois: Bahá'í Publishing Trust, 1957.

——*Selections from the Writings of 'Abdu'l-Bahá*. Translated by a Committee at the Bahá'í World Centre and by Marzieh Gail. Haifa: Bahá'í World Centre, 1987.

——*Some Answered Questions*. Collected and translated from the Persian by Laura Clifford Barney. Wilmette, Illinois: Bahá'í Publishing Trust, 1981.

Ardrey, Robert. *African Genesis: A Personal Investigation into the Animal Origins and Nature of Man*. New York: Dell Publishing Company, 1961.

——*The Territorial Imperative: A Personal Inquiry into the Animal Origins of Property and Nations*. London: Collins, The Fontana Library, 1967.

Bahá'í Revelation: A Selection from the Bahá'í Holy Writings. London: Bahá'í Publishing Trust, 1955.

Bahá'u'lláh. *Gleanings from the Writings of Bahá'u'lláh*. Translated by Shoghi Effendi. Wilmette, Illinois: Bahá'í Publishing Trust, 1963.

——*The Hidden Words of Bahá'u'lláh*. Translated by Shoghi Effendi with the assistance of some English friends. Wilmette, Illinois: Bahá'í Publishing Trust, 1954.

——*Tablets of Bahá'u'lláh revealed after the Kitáb-i-Aqdas*. Compiled by the Research Department of the Universal House of Justice and translated by HabibTaherzadeh with the assistance of a Committee at the Bahá'í World Centre, Haifa: Bahá'í World Centre, 1978.

Beyond War: Selected Resources. Palo Alto, Calif.: Beyond War, 1985.

Capra, Fritjof. *The Turning Point: Science, Society and the Rising Culture*. New York: Simon and Schuster, 1982.

Clark, William C. 'Managing Planet Earth', *Scientific American*, September 1989.

de Cuellar, Perez. *Annual Report to the United Nations General Assembly*. New York: United Nations, September 1988.

Frankl, Viktor, *Man's Search for Meaning*. New York: Beacon Press, 1959.

——*The Unconscious God*. New York: Simon and Schuster, 1975.

Frayer, David W., Horton, William A., Macchiarelli, Roberto and Mussi, Margherita. *Nature*. vol. 330, 5 November 1987.

Ghiglieri, Michael P. 'The Social Ecology of Chimpanzees', *Scientific American*. vol. 252, June 1985.

Goodall, Jane. *The Chimpanzees of Gombe: Patterns of Behavior*. Cambridge, Mass.: Belknap Press of the Harvard University Press, 1986.

The Heaven of Divine Wisdom. Compiled by the Universal House of Justice. Oakham: Bahá'í Publishing Trust, 1978.

Hobbs, Thomas. *The Leviathan or The Matter, Form and Power of a Commonwealth, Ecclesiastical and Civil*. 1651.

Hornby, Helen. *Lights of Guidance: A Bahá'í Reference File*. New Delhi, India: Bahá'í Publishing Trust, 1983.

Isaac, Glyn. 'The Food-Sharing Behavior of Protohominids', *Scientific American*, April 1979.

Lancaster, Jane Beckman. *Primate Behavior and the Emergence of Human Culture*. New York: Holt, Rinehart and Winston, 1975.

Leakey, Richard. *Human Origins*. London: Hamish Hamilton, 1982.

——*The Making of Mankind*. New York: E.P. Dutton, 1981.

Lovejoy, C. Owen. 'The Evolution of Human Walking', *Scientific American*, November 1988.

Macy, Joanna. *Despair and Personal Power in the Nuclear Age.* Philadelphia: New Society Publishers, 1983.

Menuhin, Yehudi. *Unfinished Journey*. New York: Macdonald and Jane's Publishers, 1977.

Mesarovic, Mihajlo and Pestel, Eduard. *Mankind at the Turning Point: The Second Report to the Club of Rome.* London: Hutchinson, 1975.

Montagu, Ashley (ed.). *Man and Aggression*. New York: Oxford University Press, 1968.

Moody, Raymond, A., Jr. *The Light Beyond*. New York: Bantam Books, 1988.

Morgan, Elaine, *The Aquatic Ape.* New York: Souvenir Press, 1982.

Peace: A Compilation. Compiled by the Research Department of the Universal House of Justice, Bahá'í World Centre. Oakham: Bahá'í Publishing Trust, 1985.

Reischauer, Edwin O. *Toward the 21st Century: Education for a Changing World.* New York: Alfred A. Knopf, 1974.

Robertson, Ian. *Sociology*. New York: Worth Publishers, Inc., 3rd ed. 1987.

Russell, Bertrand. *Has Man a Future?* New York: Simon and Schuster, 1962.

Salk, Jonas. 'A Conversation', *Psychology Today*, March 1983.

Sealth, Chief (Seattle) of Washington State. Address to a delegation of white men who wished to purchase his people's tribal lands, 1854.

Schell, Jonathan. *The Fate of the Earth.* New York: Alfred A. Knopf, 1982.

Shoghi Effendi. *God Passes By.* Wilmette, Illinois: Bahá'í Publishing Trust, 1944.

——*The Promised Day is Come*. Wilmette, Illinois: Bahá'í Publishing Trust, 1961.

——*The World Order of Bahá'u'lláh*. Wilmette, Illinois: Bahá'í Publishing Trust, 1969.

Tanner, Nancy Makepeace. *On Becoming Human*. Cambridge: Cambridge University Press, 1981.

Thomas, Lewis. 'Are We Fit to Fit In?', *Amicus Journal*, Summer 1981.

U Thant. *Portfolio for Peace: Excerpts from the Writings and Speeches of U Thant, Secretary-General of the United Nations, on Major World Issues, 1961–1968*. New York: United Nations, 1968.

The Universal House of Justice. *The Promise of World Peace*. Haifa: Bahá'í World Centre, 1985.

The World Commission on Environment and Development. *Our Common Future*. Oxford: Oxford University Press, 1987.

The publisher acknowledges with gratitude permission to print the illustrations appearing in the chapters listed below: Bahá'í International News Service, chapter 9; Bahá'í World Centre, frontispiece, chapters 9, 11, 16, 19; The Gorilla Foundation, chapter 8; International Labour Office, facing chapter 1, chapters 7, 17; NASA, chapter 5; Oxford Scientific Films Ltd, chapters 8, 9; Red Cross, facing chapter 13; Save the Children, chapters 4, 7, 9, 11, 16, 17, 19; Unicef, chapters 4, 5, 11, 16, 19. Richard Boyle, chapters 8, 9; Moojan Momen, chapter 11; Wendi Momen, chapter 19; Shahram Mottahed, chapter 5; Steve Worth, chapter 16.